SWORDS FROM
PUBLIC COLLECTIONS
IN THE
COMMONWEALTH
OF PENNSYLVANIA

---

with new information
regarding swordmakers
of the Philadelphia area

Bruce S. Bazelon, *Editor*

Bruce Bazelon, *Editor*
Swords from Public Collections in the Commonwealth of Pennsylvania
Lincoln, RI: ANDREW MOWBRAY INCORPORATED — *PUBLISHERS*

ISBN: 0-917218-26-4

Printed in the United States of America

Introduction

This work is intended to bring important specimens to the attention of collectors and researchers in the field of arms and technology. Its two parts show the importance of institutional collections of historical artifacts and of the records accompanying such collections. While it is true that no collector will have the thrill of purchasing and owning these specimens, their presence in public collections provides a sense of continuity with their original owners in their historical communities. Because of this context, history accompanying the pieces from the original donors can be recorded by the museum and arranged in files which document the object's "rites of passage" in the institution's collections. These records will provide a jumping off place for future students and a permanent repository for what has already been learned.

Museums have the responsibility of researching their holdings as a part of the exhibits story they must tell or as a part of the legacy which they are to pass on to future generations along with the artifacts themselves. If the original donor has supplied some of that history, so much the better, but family tradition must always be checked against the written word. The second part of this work began as just such an effort.

In 1986, the State Museum of Pennsylvania prepared an exhibit entitled the Philadelphia sword, and one great example of such a piece is the sword presented to Jonathan Goddard Watmough by Edmund Gaines. We had learned from the donor that the believed recipient of the sword was Pendleton Gaines Watmough, who began a long Naval career as a midshipman in 1841. The sword was neither Naval regulations nor typical of the 1840s. Cleaning the blade revealed the presentation inscription to the father of the midshipman but presented another problem. The sword was for gallantry in action at Fort Erie in October of 1815. Now the sword was no more typical of 1815 than of 1841, and there our search began.

John Giblin and Iris Wood were assigned the task of documenting the Watmough sword so that we could at least write an accurate label. After several months of study, a good deal of sweat and some excellent luck we knew that the sword was presented in the Fall of 1830 when Watmough was running for Congress by his old commander, General Gaines. Along with this information emerged documentation of William Rose & Sons, the blade maker; John Meer, the engraver; and Harvey Lewis, the designer. The latter figure did not even sign the sword but was mentioned in the presentation broadside as having executed its design. Thus we not only learned a good deal about Rose and his workshop, but also about how presentation swords were fabricated. Of the three marks on the sword, none were actually responsible for the appearance of more than their own piece of the artifact and they were working from a plan provided by a fourth individual whose name appeared nowhere.

Many collectors give their specimens the same care as do museums, and certainly show a great deal more love than an institution is capable of evidencing through cold publications and exhibits. But museums do play a role in our understanding of the past and its ways. They provide a standard, both in terms of quality and permanence of research. Museums often have an understanding of historical sources which most collectors have not been shown. The museum also provides a stability of location which confers a knowledge that the piece can be examined along with its historical files by containing the institution. At the same time, pieces often wait years between exhibits and the interested public has no knowledge that the piece is even in the museum. It is hoped that published catalogs such as the present effort will help to remedy that situation. In this spirit, the author wishes to thank the staff members of the participating institutions in this catalog for the cooperation they have shown and the time they have spent in the belief that this work would provide a useful document.

Bruce S. Bazelon —Editor

CONTRIBUTING INSTITUTIONS

Atwater Kent Museum (Philadelphia)

The Atwater Kent Museum was founded in 1939 and houses the historical collections of the City of Philadelphia. Its collections consist of materials relating to Philadelphia, among which are a number of fine military colors and weapons.
Photo Credit: Mr. Donnie Roberts   Director: Mr. John Alviti

The Chester County Historical Society (West Chester)

The Chester County Historical Society was organized in 1893 by a group of prominent local citizens, including several internationally known scientists and authors. Dr. Joseph T. Rothrock, explorer and conservationist was elected the first president. The purpose of the Society, stated by the Charter, is "the acquisition and preservation of property and information of historic value or interest to the people of Chester County."

In 1941, the Society opened its first permanent home — the building designed by Thomas U. Walter for the Chester County Horticultural Society, which was completed in 1848. The over 50,000 items in the collections of the Society's museum contain outstanding examples of the region's decorative, useful and fine arts. Particularly remarkable are the furniture, costumes, needlework and textiles, pewter, glass and ceramics. The library is equally rich with over 20,000 books, extensive manuscripts, newspaper files and maps. In August, 1982, The Chester County Archives / Dorothy B. Lapp Research Center opened at the Chester County Courthouse, a joint venture between the Society and the county government.
Photo Credit: Mr. George Fistrovich   Curators: Ms. Ann Brown; Ms. Margaret Bleecker Blades

First Regiment Infantry Museum (Philadelphia)

The First Regiment Infantry of the National Guard of Pennsylvania traces its direct lineage to the Grey Reserves of the Civil War and to the Washington Grays Artillery founded in 1823. These units in turn carry on the heritage of still older organizations including pre-Revolutionary Pennsylvania 'Associators'. The unit remains in the Pennsylvania National Guard as the 103d Combat Engineer Battalion. Its museum and archives contain collections associated with the important role it has played in Pennsylvania's Military History.
Photo Credit: SFC Peter Willcox   Director: MAJ J. Craig Nannos

Historical Society of Pennsylvania (Philadelphia)

Founded in 1824, the 'HSP' is one of the oldest historical institutions in the United States. The society maintains a 100,000 volume research library and encyclopedic manuscript holdings which include many documents of extraordinary importance to national as well as Pennsylvania history. Its object collections consist of historical portraits and decorative arts materials dating from the seventeenth to the twentieth centuries. It has a small, but very fine military collection consisting of weapons, uniforms and colors.
Photo Credit: Mr. Lewis Meehan   Director: Mr. Peter Parker

The Mercer Museum of the Bucks County Historical Society (Doylestown)

Founded in 1880, this museum represents the collecting efforts of Henry Chapman Mercer in pre-industrial era tools and products. The museum also houses the collections of the Bucks County Historical Society through whose collecting efforts many of the well documented

swords and uniforms have been gathered. The museum also houses a 12,000 volume research library related to Bucks County Pennsylvania.
Photo Credit: Mr. James R. Blackaby   Curator: Mr. James R. Blackaby

Mifflin County Historical Society (Lewistown)

The Mifflin County Historical Society is housed in the General Frank McCoy House, maintained by the Pennsylvania Historical and Museum Commission. The collections owned by the society consist of important memoribilia of General Frank McCoy, one of America's leading soldier diplomats of the early twentieth century and general history collections related to Mifflin County, Pennsylvania. The society also maintains a library and publications program.
Photo credit: Mr. Terry Musgrave

Pennsylvania Historical and Museum Commission

The PHMC is the historical agency of the Commonwealth of Pennsylvania and as such administers a network of some sixty historic sites and museums throughout Pennsylvania. The William Penn Memorial Museum (the State Museum) in Harrisburg is the largest of these holdings and it is from the collections of the WPMM that the swords described have been drawn. The military holdings of the Commonwealth exist from the Revolution as some items in the collections have never left state ownership.
Photo Credit: Mr. Terry Musgrave   Curator: Mr. Bruce S. Bazelon

Pottstown Historical Society (Pottstown)

This historical society is headquartered in Pottsgrove Mansion which it furnishes in conjunction with the PHMC. The society also maintains collections related to the Pottstown area, included in which is a small military collection, now in storage.
Photo Credit: Mr. Terry Musgrave   President: Mr. Raymond P. Elliott

Schuylkill County Historical Society (Pottsville)

The Schuylkill County Historical Society represents Pottsville's important military past in its collections. Artifacts range from uniforms to weapons and musical instruments and date from the early nineteenth century through the middle twentieth.
Curator: Mr. Russell Hirshberger

Union League (Philadelphia)

Founded by Union sympathizers in 1862, the Union League has been a major civic, patriotic and political force in Philadelphia. While a private organization, its holdings consist of a major research library, an archive of military and political history, an art collection and objects of military interest deposited by members over the past century.
Photo Credit: Mr. Terry Musgrave   Historical Consultant: Mr. Maxwell Whiteman

Wyoming Historical and Geological Society (Wilkes-Barre)

The Wyoming Historical and Geological Society is one of the oldest historical institutions in Northeastern Pennsylvania. Its collections consist of historical and scientific specimens from the Wilkes-Barre area and the anthracite coal region. The society has a fine military collection of documented uniforms, arms, and a highly significant collection of unit colors from the area.
Photo Credit: Mr. Joseph Sgromo   Curator: Mr. Joseph Sgromo

Table of Contents

SWORD PRESENTATION.

A Sword and Sash prepared for Presentation to Col. George C. Wynkoop, of the Seventh Pennsylvania Cavalry, by his citizen-friends of Pottsville, will be presented to that gallant officer at the

TOWN HALL, POTTSVILLE,

ON THURSDAY EVENING, MAY 7, 1863, AT 8 O'CLOCK.

☞ The public is respectfully invited to attend.

FRONT SEATS RESERVED FOR LADIES.

JOHN BANNAN,
JOHN SHIPPEN,
BURD PATTERSON,
R. R. MORRIS,
A. RUSSEL,
JAS. H. CAMPBELL,

D. G. YUENGLING,
ALEX. MOORHEAD,
WM. FOX,
JNO. CLAYTON,
WM. WOLFF,
SOLOMON FOSTER,

S. N. PALMER,

Committee of Arrangements.

POTTSVILLE, MAY 5, 1863.

Preface to Part I

One criticism often leveled towards museums having military collections is that fine specimens are often relegated to storage and thus remain unknown to those having an interest in the study of arms. While this criticism is in part deserved, it is also true that museums provide a steady place of reference towards their collections and can at the same time record the history and circumstances of an object as known to the donor at the time of presentation. Such knowledge as to the location and history of a piece can be all too easily obliterated by sale or death were the object to remain in private hands.

Because museums have reference collections which are in some part documented, it is especially important these specimens be brought to the attention of those interested in learning about their holdings.

The present work represents the cooperative effort of some ten institutions in the eastern half of Pennsylvania to see important pieces from their collections brought to the attention of those who should know that these specimens exist. While some of the pieces depicted are indeed in storage at present, the majority can be seen in exhibit at their various homes.

Bruce S. Bazelon —*Editor*

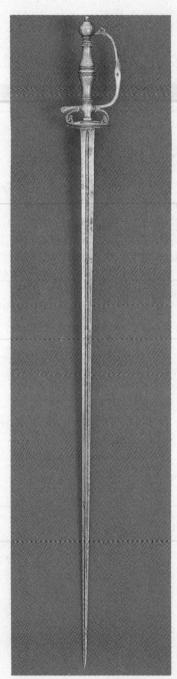

CONGRESSIONAL PRESENTATION SWORD TO COLONEL TENCH TILGHMAN

Inscription: (on grip) Presented/to/Lieut. Col. / Tench Tilghman/by the/Continental Congress/ in Appreciation/ of his Merit/and Service. Marks: Touch (R.H.) of Richard Humphreys, Philadelphia silversmith (1750-1832).

Tench Tilghman of Philadelphia was Aide de Camp and Military Secretary to George Washington through most of the Revolution. His services were recognized by an act of Congress on 29 October, 1781. It was "Resolved that the Board of War be directed to present to Lieutenant Colonel Tilghman, in the name of the United States, in Congress assembled, a horse properly caparisoned, and an elegant sword, in testimony of their high opinion of his merit and ability."

The present sword, while only one of a number awarded by Congress, is considered to be the only such piece known to have been made in America. However, Tilghman was to have been the recipient of one of the ten presentation swords made by Liger in Paris for those officers cited in Acts of Congress during the Revolution. These swords were manufactured in 1785, but Tilghman's did not reach him before his death in 1786. This French-made sword is now in the Anderson House Museum of the Society of the Cincinnati. As the sword cited in this book was apparently given to the Atwater Kent Museum by a member of the Philadelphia branch of Tilghman's family and dates from the approximate period of the Revolution, it is apparently a second sword. Any explanation as to its existence is conjectural, but it is possible that, as five years elapsed between the Act of Congress in 1781 and the delivery of the French-made piece, a sword was made or used by Tilghman as an interim piece.

Courtesy: Atwater Kent Museum 77.742

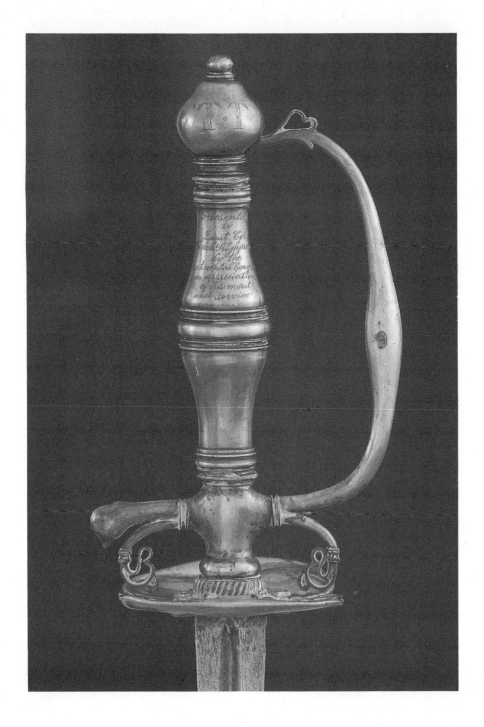

HORSEMAN'S SABER, PHILADELPHIA, ca. 1780

This saber was received by the State Museum in Harrisburg from a local GAR Post in 1929 with no indication as to its past history or ownership. The one piece brass hilt is typical of Philadelphia sword-smithing. The pommel is in the "dog's head" motif and the 34¾" blade is hand drawn from a single piece of steel. The guard was recently restored by Mr. Kit Ravenshear, which process involved rebuilding one entire side which had broken off.

Courtesy: Pennsylvania Historical and Museum Commission 29.6.251.

12

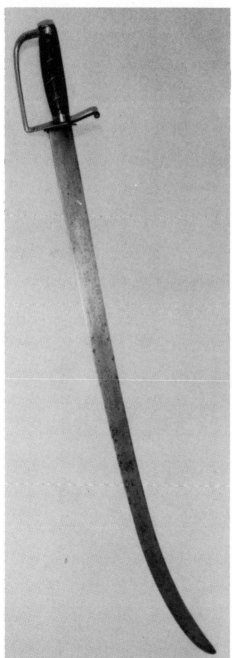

HORSEMAN'S SABER, ca. 1780

This plain ironmounted saber is typical of the mounted swords of the Revolutionary cavalryman. It has wooden grips reinforced by an iron backstrap and a twisted wire wrap. The blade is flat and has no fuller.

Courtesy: Mercer Museum

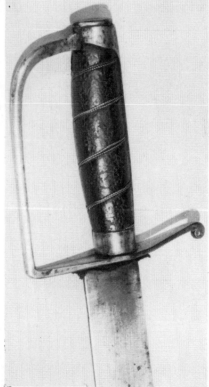

PRESENTATION SWORD TO
COLONEL JOHN WITHY

Inscription: "Vive 'le Roy"; Maker's Mark: "I·J" (top edge of scabbard)
Overall length: 37¼". Blade length: 30¼".

According to family history, this sword was originally owned by Col. John Withy, and was presented to the Colonel by General Howe. The mark is that of John Jenkins, a Revolutionary War period Philadelphia silversmith.   *Chester County Historical Society, West Chester, PA; Photographs by George Fistrovich*

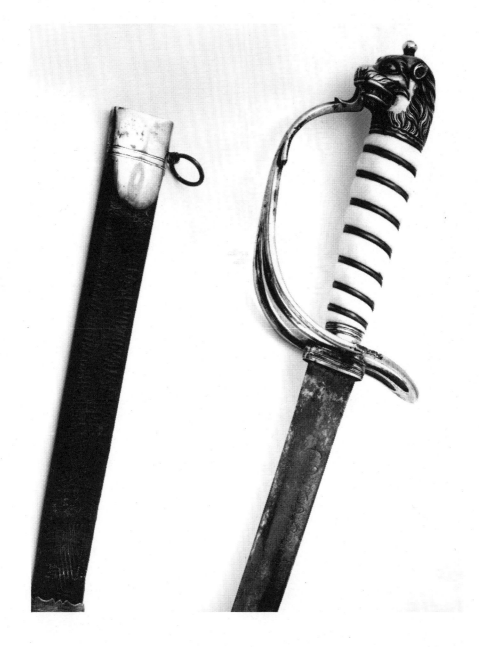

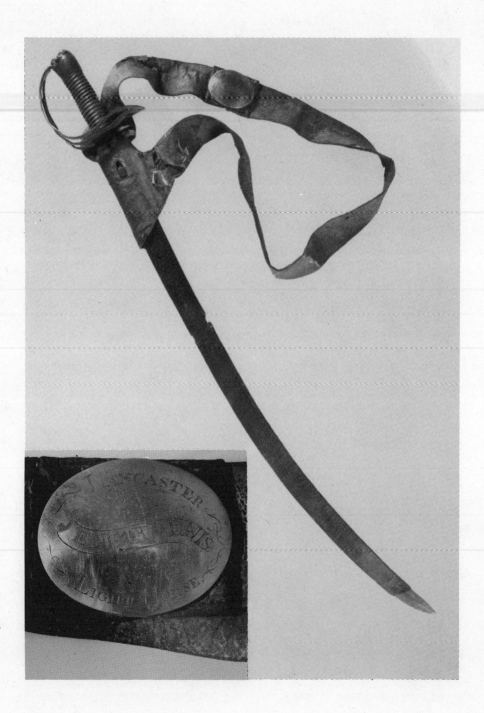

HORSEMAN'S SABER OF EDWARD DAVIS
LANCASTER COUNTY LIGHT HORSE, ca. 1795.

Inscription: (on saber belt plate) LANCASTER/EDWARD DAVIS/LIGHT HORSE.

This saber with brass hilt and "lion's head" pommel is documented by the presence of the original saber belt and silver plate which remains attached to the sword scabbard. Davis appears on a militia fine list for delinquencies incurred as a member of the 4th Division (Lancaster County), Pennsylvania Militia between 1793-1795. These dates are approximately those which can be attributed for this sword on stylistic grounds.

The blade is marked "ROSE" on the quill.   *Courtesy: Pottstown Historical Society*

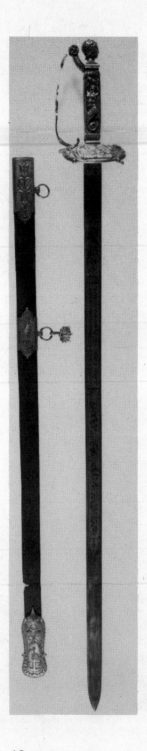

CONGRESSIONAL PRESENTATION SWORD TO GEORGE SENAT, 1814

Inscription: (on blade) GEORGE SENAT Midshipman Comm./Lake Erie, 10th September 1813.
— ALTIUS IBUNT QUI AD SUMMA NITUNTUR
Maker: W. Rose (on reverse ricasso)
Engraver: MEER Philadelphia (John Meer — on obverse ricasso).

Each commander of a vessel which took part in the actions surrounding Perry's victory on Lake Erie received a sword from Congress. This piece, like the other swords in this presentation, was made by William Rose and magnificently etched by John Meer. The recipient, George Senat, commanded the USS Porcupine, 1 gun, and was a midshipman in the Navy.

Courtesy: Historical Society of Pennsylvania P-7-14.

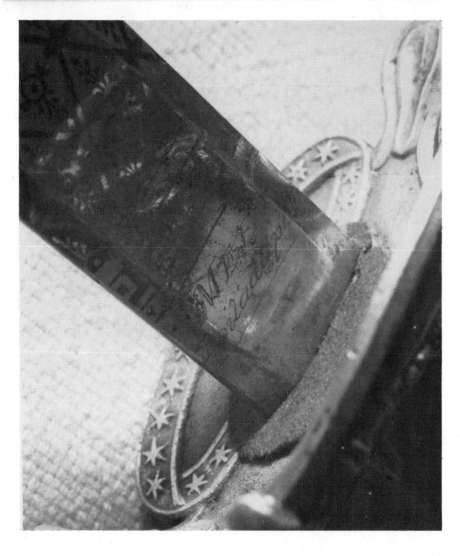

PRESENTATION SWORD TO
JONATHAN GODDARD WATMOUGH
FROM MAJOR GENERAL EDMUND P. GAINES,
1830

This silver hilted eagle head pommel sword is known to have been designed by the silversmith Harvey K. Lewis of Philadelpia and is one of a number of swords designed by this craftsman. The blade is signed W. Rose and was decorated by John Meer with a scene of General Gaines "...directing the attack on the enemy... at the same time curbing his charger, and leaning down towards a wounded officer, on the ground, supported by a soldier. The time represented is soon after the explosion of the bastion...." The scene depicts an incident which occured at the siege of Fort Erie, in August 1814, for which the sword was awarded many years later. Gaines was in command of this fort and Watmough gravely wounded in its defence. The hilt of the sword, though designed by Harvey Lewis, is marked 'J. Hub' — possibly a contraction — in spite of other silver pieces which have been noted with this mark. Hub, whoever he was, presumably was a silversmith who executed the overall hilt design.

The sword is described in a pamphlet written for Watmough's election to Congress as a Whig in 1830. The sword was presented on or about August 27, 1830 by General Cadwalader of the Philadelphia militia representing General Gaines, then commanding the US Army of the West, from whom the pamphlet describes the sword as being a spontaneous gift. (Watmough Papers, Historical Society of Pennsylvania) The sword is now in the collections of the State Museum of Pennsylvania. Gift of the Higgins family.

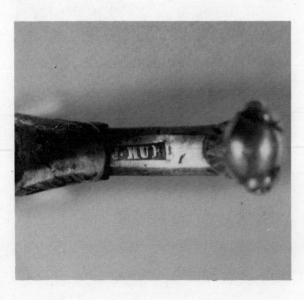

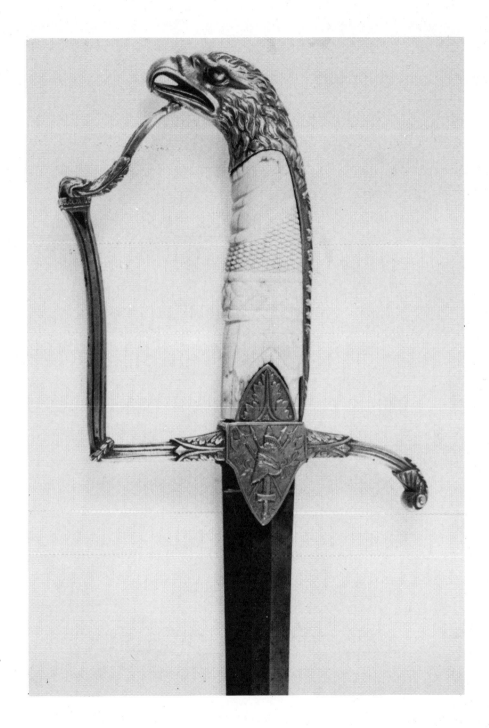

U.S. ARTILLERY SABER OF CAPTAIN WILLIAM MAGILL, BUCKS COUNTY, PENNSYLVANIA, ca. 1815

Maker: Stamped ROSE on the top of the blade near the guard.

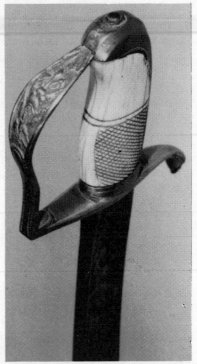

This saber descended in the family of William Magill, listed in the Pennsylvania Militia Commission book of 1821-7 as being Captain of the Independent Artillerists of Bucks County (1st Brigade, 2nd Division Pennsylvania Militia). The sword has the script letters U S of A intertwined in gilt on the blued forte of the blade. The date of the sword's manufacture should be a few years prior to Magill's first recorded service but the general style and gilting of the hilt and scabbard indicates probable artillery usage. Presented by W. Howard Magill, October 1918. *Courtesy: Mercer Museum 13498*

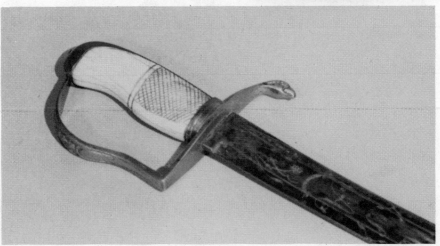

SILVER MOUNTED
EAGLE HEAD SABER
ca. 1810-1826:

This piece was purchased by the Mercer Museum in 1941 with no recorded history. It is a good example of an eagle pommel silver hilt sword, most likely intended for a militia infantry officer. The grips are of plain wood with a single twist wire wrapping. The piece is rather short at 34⅝″ overall with a 29″ blade. There are no hallmarks on the silver portions of the sword.

Courtesy Mercer Museum 25476

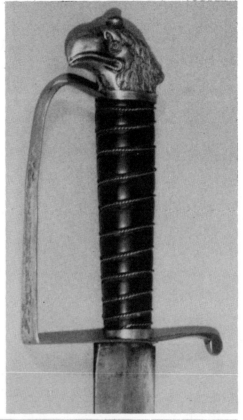

"PRAHL" TYPE SABER OF CHRISTIAN KNEASS
2ND TROOP PHILADELPHIA CITY CAVALRY, 1814

Marks: Stamped on grip: CHRISTIAN KNEASS SECOND TROOP PHILADA CAV 1814.

This saber is the only "Prahl" type sword known to have historical associations as to its original owner. The piece was donated to the 2nd Troop Philadelphia City Cavalry by Kneass's descendants in 1910. At some point the family had already stamped the name and date of the sword's original ownership into the brass grip. A muster of the troop dated October 2, 1814 confirms Kneass's membership at that date. The saber is rather short at 36½" overall with a 31½" blade.

Courtesy: Pennsylvania Historical and Museum Commission 72.241.4

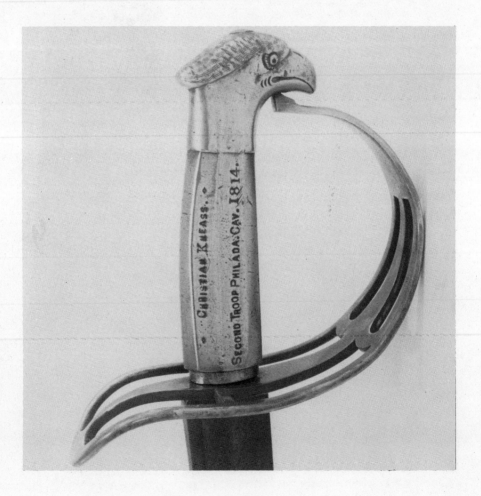

SABER PRESENTED TO
CAPT. H.G. MALLORY, 1844

Inscription: (etched on reverse of the blade) The Citizens of Philadelphia to Capt. H.G. Mallory/as a token of respect for his brave conduct and distinguished services in/Southwark on the night of the 7th of July 1844.
Marks: (2 lines on obverse ricasso) Bailey & Kitchen/ Phila.

This saber, described by Peterson as a "Mounted Artillery Officer's Saber" presents something of a mystery at present. Mallory is listed neither as a regular Army officer nor does his name appear in the Pennsylvania Commission Books as having received a Commission from the Commonwealth.
(Continued on following page)

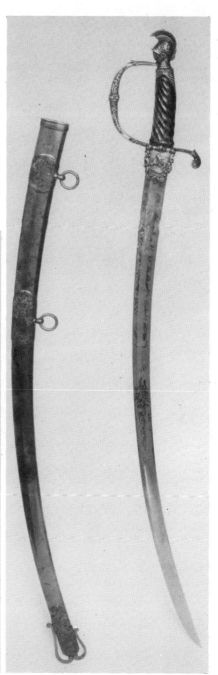

SABER PRESENTED TO CAPT. H.G. MALLORY, 1844
(Continued from previous page)

The incident for which the sword was awarded is, however, well documented. There were anti-Catholic riots in the Southwark section of Philadelphia in July, 1844, in which several serious injuries were received. Although several works have been devoted to these incidents, no mention can be found of Mallory either as a militiaman or as a fire captain. There is a Henry Mallory listed in the 1850 census as being a resident of Southwark.

The absence of Mallory on the militia roles is partially explained in the printed presentation documents which accompanied the sword's donation in 1930. These show that Mallory received the sword with two silver pitchers at a presentation ceremony in Germantown, probably in 1844. Mallory later ran for public office and explained his actions in the riots of 1844 in an attempt to gather votes. He notes that "...Having accepted the comand of a company of volunteers..." he proceeded to help quell the disturbances. The name of the company Mallory commanded appear in no record thus far available. The above reference bears the connotation that his command was of a temporary nature for this instance alone. Certainly, whatever part Mallory played in riots it was judged important by his contemporaries, but has not been noted by later sources.

Bailey & Kitchen — soon to become Bailey & Company and now known as Bailey Banks and Biddle — is a famous jewelry making firm in Philadelphia. This firm had the capacity to manufacture the fine quality hilt and scabbard on this sword as well as others cited below. Unfortunately, the records of the firm were discarded some years ago and it is impossible to prove their manufacturing capacities of the time.   *Courtesy: Historical Society of Pennsylvania P-6-10*

Opposite page:

MEXICAN WAR PRESENTATION SABER TO GEORGE A. McCALL, 1846

Inscription: (on scabbard) PALO ALTO AND RESACA DE LA PALMA, MAY 1846/CAPTAIN GEORGE A. McCALL./4th Regiment of Infantry, UNITED STATES ARMY/from his/FELLOW CITIZENS OF PHILADELPHIA. (on scabbard).

Marks: Bailey & Co./ Phila, Pa on obverse ricasso and on scabbard throat

N.P. Ames, Cutler Springfield

This magnificent presentation saber has silver scabbard and grips with gilt mountings. It was presented to a regular Army officer, George A. McCall. McCall graduated from the Military Academy in 1818 and remained a Captain until brevetted a major for his conduct at the engagements cited upon the scabbard of this sword — Palo Alto and Resaca de la Palma. McCall went on to become a Colonel in 1850 and a general officer during the Civil War (see page 40)

Courtesy: Historical Society of Pennsylvania

PRESENTATION SWORD TO FIRST LIEUTENANT T.F. McCOY 1848

Inscription: (on scabbard between rings) Presented to lst. Lieut. T.F. M'Coy, by the Non. Com./Privates and Musicians of Co.D llth U.S. Infantry. As a/token of regard for his bravery in the Field and his gentlemanly/conduct in camp. New York Augt. 1848

Marks: (etched on reverse of ricasso) Ames Mfg Co/Cabotville/Mass

Thomas F. McCoy was commissioned a First Lieutenant of Infantry on February 18, 1847. He was serving with his regiment in Mexico several months later and was brevetted captain for gallantry and meritorious conduct at Contreras and Churubusco. He resigned his commission in August, 1848 — the same month in which he was given this sword. McCoy later served as Colonel of the 107th Pennsylvania Volunteer Infantry during the Civil War. The sword was given with other McCoy military memoribilia by the family of T.F. McCoy's son, General Frank McCoy. *Courtesy: Mifflin County Historical Society*

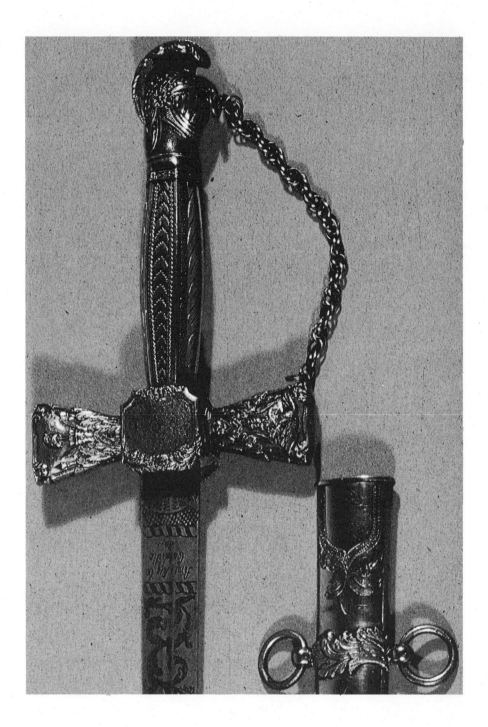

MILITIA OFFICER'S SWORD, ca. 1830-1840

Maker: F.W. Widmann (ob blade side of guard).

This militia sword is described by Peterson as a "Mounted Artillery Officer's Saber". The narrow and somewhat elongated eagle's head is typical of the Widmann style and must have been made prior to Widmann's death in 1847. No history was given by the donor on the sword's presentation to the Mercer Museum in 1922.   *Courtesy: Mercer Museum 18674.*

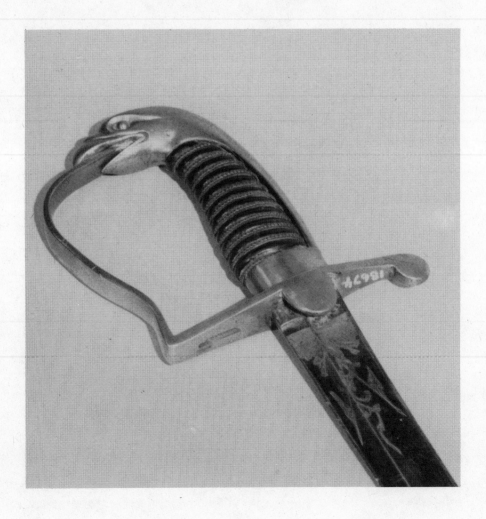

MODEL 1840 FOOT OFFICER'S SWORD PRESENTED TO W.W.H. DAVIS, 1847

Inscription: (engraved on counterguard) Presented by the Officers and Members of the Doylestown Grays to their fellow member/ W.W.H. Davis on his departure for the/Seat of War. January 30, 1847.

Marks: (engraved underneath counter guard) F.W. Widmann/Philada

This superbly etched, brass mounted sword was presented to William W.H. Davis of Bucks County, Pennsylvania. According to the sword's inscription Davis was a member of the Doylestown Grays before the Mexican War — though the official records fail to denote his exact status. When war was declared, Davis joined the First Massachusetts Infantry and served in Mexico as a Lieutenant and Captain of that unit. Returning to Doylestown from Mexico, Davis became Captain of the Diller Artillerists and later a major of the 2nd Detachment Bucks County Volunteers. During the Civil War, Davis was commissioned a Captain in the 25th Pennsylvania Volunteer Infantry (the Doylestown Guard) and was later Colonel of the 104th Pennsylvania Volunteer Infantry. The sword was donated to the Bucks County Historical Society, which Davis helped to found, by his heirs in July, 1898.

Courtesy: Mercer Museum 1514.

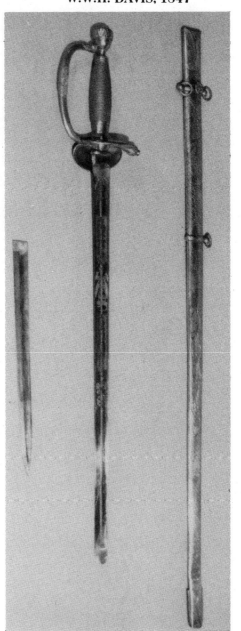

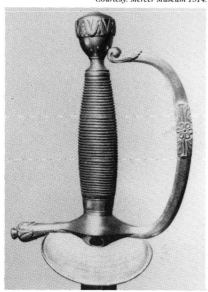

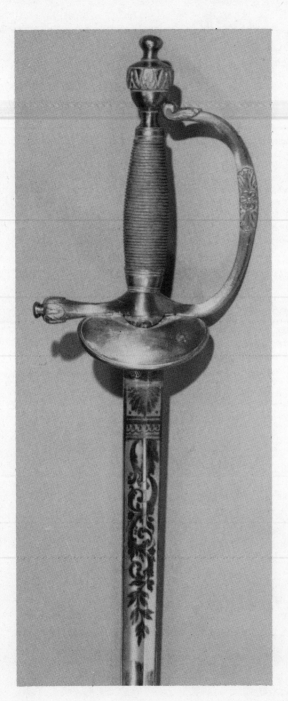

MODEL 1840 FOOT OFFICERS SWORD OF GENERAL APPLEBACH

This sword is very similar to the Davis sword cited above. Its only mark is the crowned head attributed to Solingen on the blade. The two swords differ only in such details as the pommel nut, which is found in an elongated version in the Applebach sword. As the Davis sword was made in the year of Widmann's death (1847) and with the Widmann dies being purchased by Horstmann the next year, it is probable that the piece is of Horstmann manufacture.

Paul Applebach (Applebaugh) is listed in the Pennsylvania Commission book of 1854-1854 as a Major General commanding the 2nd Division of Pennsylvania Militia. Although he was still in this position when the Civil War broke out, he has no known war service.

Courtesy: Mercer Museum

PRESENTATION SWORD TO PETER FRITZ, 1852

Major Peter Fritz was a well known figure in the Philadelphia militia before the Civil War. He is probably cited in the Commission book of 1807-1810 as a First Lieutenant in the Artillery Regiment of the First Division. While this first citation could be that of a relative, our Peter Fritz is found as a Lieutenant in the State Fencibles during the middle 1820's. He also appears during this period as Captain of the National Grays, a company he commanded thru June of 1861. He was Colonel of the 99th Pennsylvania Volunteer Infantry from February thru June of 1862 and had been a Captain in the 3 month 18th Pennsylvania Volunteer Infantry. His son, also Peter Fritz, later became Colonel of the 99th in 1864-1865.

Inscription: (on obverse of gilt brass scabbard) To/ Major Peter Fritz/ of Philadelphia/ from his Military friends in the City of New York/ as a token of their high Esteem for him as a / Citizen and as a Soldier. (On reverse of scabbard) By/ I.W. Downing/ P.V. Mundon/ T. Thomas/ M.D. Greene/ Committee/ Presented Feb. 12th, 1852.

Marks: (on reverse throat of scabbard) Made for/Wm H. Smith & Co./by/Ames Mfg. Co./ Chicopee,/ Mass. (on reverse ricasso, die stamped) Ames/ Mfg. Co./ Chicopee/ Mass.

The William H. Smith Company of New York was one of the great military importing and retailing houses of the period. It was begun by Henry Young and his brother-in-law, William H Smith, in 1821 and went through several evolutions as Young, Smith & Co, Young & Smith Smith Crane & Co and eventually as Shannon Miller & Crane (1866). The importance of this sword is that it shows clearly the chain of sale from actual manufacturer to retailer and then to customer.

Courtesy: War Library and Museum MOLLUS

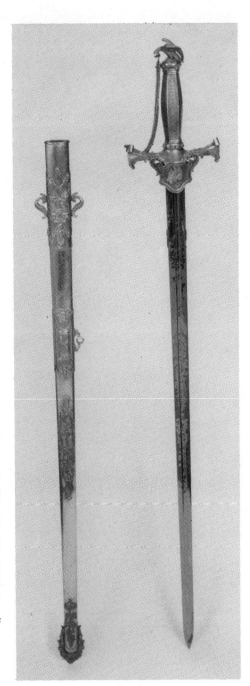

MEXICAN SABER PRESENTED TO COL. FRANCIS WYNKOOP
1st REGIMENT PENNSYLVANIA VOLUNTEERS, 1847

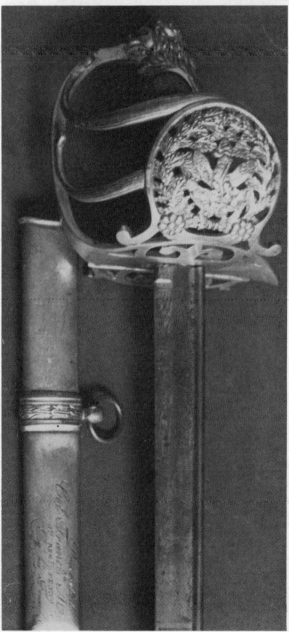

Description: Mexican saber with straight French made etched blade having a pronounced quill. The branched guard incorporates the Mexican arms and a folding counterguard. The pommel features a lion's head. The inscription is engraved upon the German silver scabbard which in turn is mounted with brass furniture. Blade 34"; overall 41".

Inscription: Presented / to / Col. Francis M. Wynkoop / 1st REGT PENN VOL / by his friend Francis Loret.

Courtesy: Schuylkill County Historical Society

PRESENTATION SWORD TO
COLONEL PETER H. ALLABACH, 1862

Maker's Marks: "W.H. / HORSTMANN / & SONS / PHILADELPHIA"

The Allabach sword is mounted in a special glass top case together with his shoulder straps, Mexican War medal, Civil War corps insignia and sash. The sword was presented to Allabach by the Reverend James Calder of Harrisburg in 1862.

Allabach (born in Willkes-Barre, PA, in 1824 and died in Washington, DC, in 1892) served in the Mexican War with Company A, 3rd U.S. Infantry, from Nov. 25, 1844 to Nov. 25, 1849.

Allabach's Civil War service was as Colonel of the nine month 131st Pennsylvania Volunteer Infantry from Aug. 18, 1862 thru May 23, 1863. In this short timespan, the regiment engaged in such battles as Fredericksburg and Chancellorsville. *Courtesy: Wyoming Historical & Geological Society*

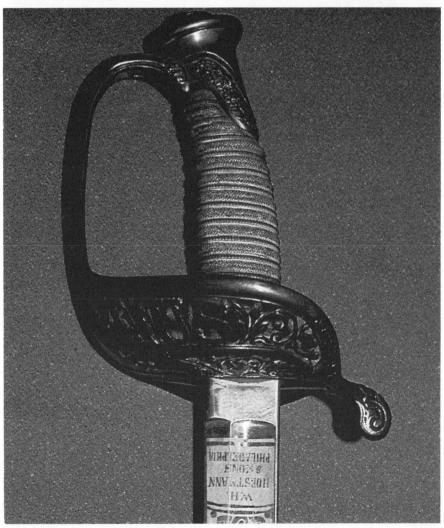

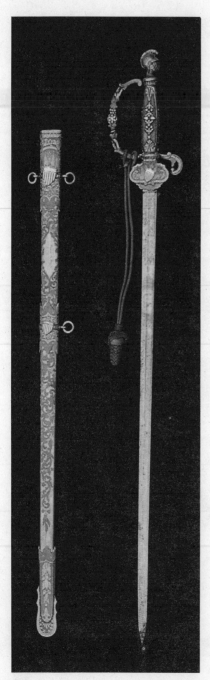

ARMY PRESENTATION SWORD TO GENERAL G.G. MEADE, 1864

This superb quality presentation sword was given to General Meade "... from the Great Central Fair Philadelphia, June 1864." This Fair represented an enormous patriotic celebration in Philadelphia whose receipts were to go to the U.S. Sanitary Commission. The Fair opened on June 7, 1864, and was visited by President Lincoln on the 16th. "A Magnificent $2500 Sword was presented to General Meade the hero of Gettysburg, who was voted the visitors' favorite general."*

Inscription: Two scabbards-both engraved 'MAJOR GENERAL/George G. Meade,/ from the Great Central Fair/ Philadelphia, June 1864.'

Marks: (on obverse ricasso) Evans & Hassall/ Philada
        Knight's head (Solingen) mark
(On inside lid of presentation box) Evans & Hassall, Phila.

Evans & Hassall was a Civil War military goods retailing firm. It began as an offshoot of the W.H. Horstmann & Sons Company, and , so far as is known, posessed no manufacturing capacity for the production of metal trimmings. The firm was reorganized several times in the late 1860s finally emerging as J.H. Wilson after 1870.

Courtesy: Historical Society of Pennsylvania

*Edwin Wolf, *Philadelphia Portrait of an American City* (Stackpole Books, Harrisburg, 1974), p. 219.

PRESENTATION SWORD TO GENERAL D.B. BIRNEY, 1862

Inscription: (on scabbard) Gen. D.B. Birney/ October, 1862/ From his Fellow Citizens of Philadelphia

Marks: Bailey & Co./ Philada (on obverse ricasso)

David Bell Birney was the son of an anti-slavery leader from Huntsville, Alabama. The family relocated in the North when Birney was a child. He moved to Philadelphia in 1856. Birney began his Civil War career as Lieutenant Colonel of the 23rd Pennsylvania Volunteer Infantry and was, by 1864, a Major General commanding the X Army Corps. He died of malaria in October, 1864.

The Birney presentation sword is distinguished, like many Bailey Civil War swords, by the use of 'hard paste enamel' (cloisonne) to pick out detail on portions of the hilt. The Bailey firm was one of a very few manufacturers of jewelry to employ this technique in the 1860's.

Courtesy: Historical Society of Pennsylvania P-3-5

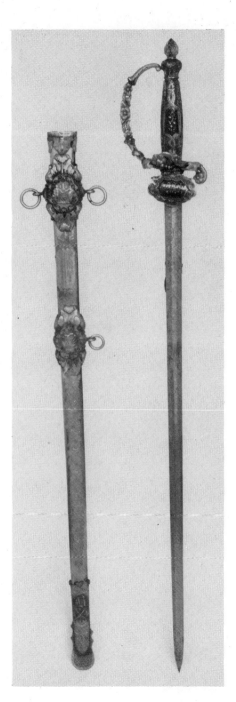

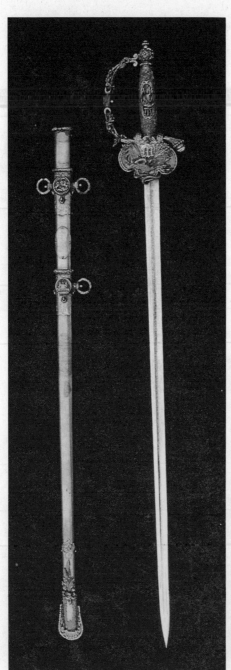

PRESENTATION SWORD TO MAJOR GENERAL GEORGE G. MEADE, 1864

Inscriptions (oval plaque between ring mounts) THE CITY/ OF PHILADELPHIA/ TO/ MAJOR GENERAL/ Geo. G. Meade/ February 22nd/ 1864. (Below lower ring mount on scabbard) In grateful/ Acknowledgement/ of the deliverance of/ Pennsylvania from/ Rebel invasion by the/ matchless valour of/ the Army which helped/ to signal victory on/ the memorable field/ of Gettysburg/ July 3rd 1863.

Marks: Clauberg over Solingen each in an arc, struck on the obverse ricasso.

While there is no manufacturer's mark for the fittings of this important sword, there is a good probability that the actual source of the sword was Bailey & Company because of the presence of the hard paste enamel work on the scabbard and guard. It is quite similar to another Meade sword at the War Library and Museum which is Bailey marked (see page 44). *Courtesy: Historical Society of Pennsylvania P-6-7*

PRESENTATION SWORD TO MAJOR GENERAL A.A. HUMPHREYS, 1865

Inscription: (on oval plaque located between the ring mounts of the scabbard) Presented to/ Major General/ A.A. Humphreys U.S.A./ by his fellow citizens of Philadelphia/ 1865

Marks: Clauberg over Solingen each in an arc, struck on the obverse ricasso.

Andrew Atkinson Humphreys was a professional soldier, graduating from the Military Academy in 1831, who was a major in the Topographical Engineers in 1861. He was a brigadier general of volunteers in 1862 and a major general of volunteers in 1863. He was General Meade's chief of staff and was a division commander in the V Corps, Army of the Potomac and later a Corps commander (II Corps). After the war he was made Brigadier General and Chief of Engineers.

Courtesy: Historical Society of Pennsylvania P-7-9

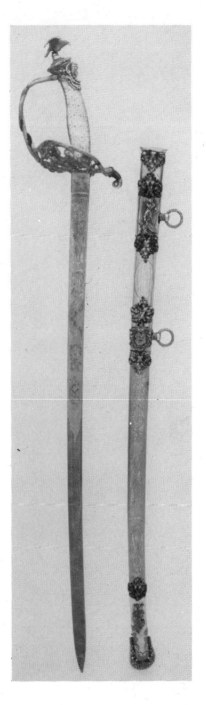

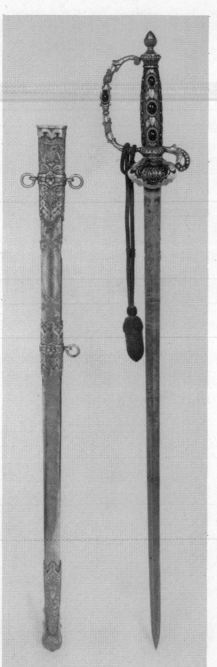

PRESENTATION SWORD TO GENERAL GEORGE A. McCall, 1862

Inscription: (on scabbard) FROM/ CITIZENS OF CHESTER COUNTY, PA./ HIS NEIGHBORS AND FRIENDS/ TO/ GEN. GEORGE A McCALL/ 1862

Marks: Bailey and Co./ Philada (on obverse ricasso)

Another Bailey presentation sword was given to George A. McCall. At the outbreak of the War McCall, who graduated from the Military Academy in 1822, was living in retirement on his farm in Chester County, Pennsylvania. He had served in the Seminole and Mexican Wars as a regular officer and he at once volunteered his services. McCall was made a Major General of Volunteers and was placed in command of "the Pennsylvania Reserves". He was taken prisoner in June of 1862 at Glendale and remained in captivity for two months until exchanged. Upon his release McCall returned home on sick leave and resigned from the Army in March, 1863.

Courtesy: Historical Society of Pennsylvania P-7-lOB

PRESENTATION QUALITY SWORD OF COLONEL GEORGE R. ORME

Inscription: none

Marks: Clauberg Solingen each in an arc on the obverse ricasso

There is no inscription on this high quality presentation sword nor is there any knowledge of the circumstances of Ormes career for which he would have merited such a presentation. He was commissioned a captain in May of 1864, but was later brevetted a lieutenant colonel and then a colonel of volunteers. Orme's entire service seems to have been as a staff quartermaster. He was mustered out in November, 1866.

Courtesy: Historical Soceity of Pennsylvania P-7-12

ARMY PRESENTATION SWORD TO MAJOR GENERAL FRANCIS P. BLAIR
1862

Inscription: (engraved between ring mounts of the scabbard) Presented to/ General Francis P. Blair by the Union Ladies of St. Louis./ 1862.

Marks. Dailey & Co./ Chestnut Street/ Philadelphia (etched on obverse ricasso); W. Clauberg/ Solingen (stamped in two lines on reverse ricasso)

Francis Preston Blair was the brother of Lincoln's Postmaster General and a powerful political personage in his own right. At the same time, he was a talented soldier serving with Generals Sherman and Grant in the Army of the Tennessee. He served at Vicksburg and commanded the XV and XVII Corps during Sherman's March thru Georgia and the Carolinas. After the war he ran as vice presidential candidate in 1868, and served as a Senator from Missouri.

Courtesy: War Library and Museum MOLLUS

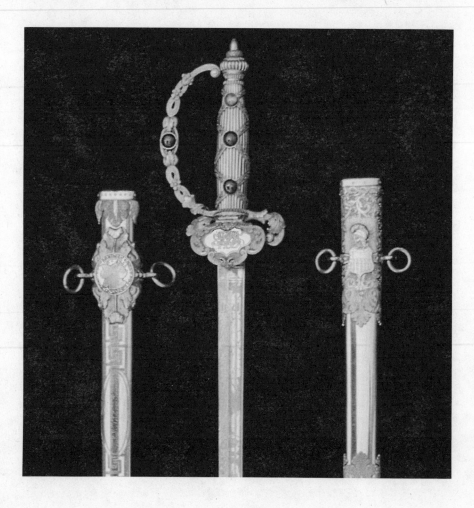

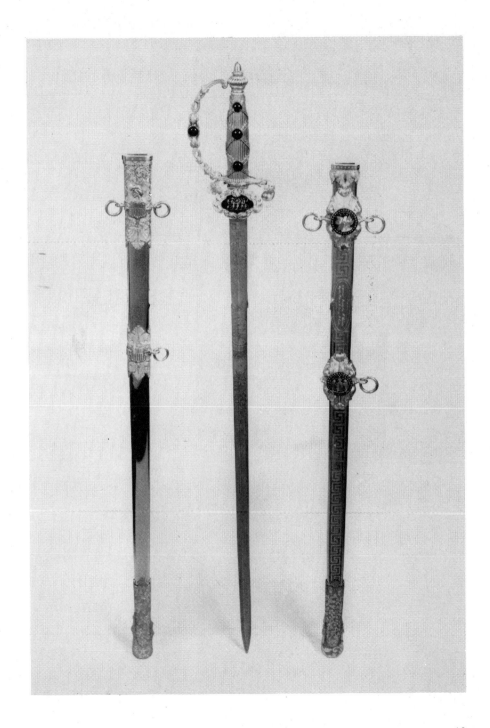

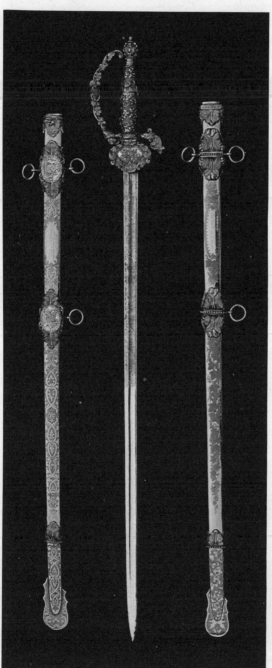

ARMY PRESENTATION SWORD TO GENERAL MEADE

Inscription: (engraved between ring mounts of the scabbard) Mechanicsville/ Gaine's Hill (sic), New Market Cross Roads/ Malverne Hill, Bull Run 2d/ South Mountain, Antietam, Fredrksburg (sic)/ Chancellorville (sic), Gettysburg

Marks: Bailey & Co./ Chestnut Street/ Philadelphia (on obverse ricasso-etched) W. Clauberg/ Solingen (stamped on reverse ricasso)

We have no knowledge of the circumstances of the presentation of this sword to General Meade. It is another very costley Bailey piece and is most curious because of the mis-spelling of the names of the engagements cited upon the scabbard.
Courtesy: War Library and Museum MOLLUS

ARMY PRESENTATION SWORD TO GENERAL ULYSSES S. GRANT 1862

Inscription: VICKSBURG (between ring mounts of the scabbard)

Marks: Schuyler/ Hartley/ &/ Graham/ New York (etched on reverse ricasso); Collins & Co./ Hartford/ Conn./ 1862. (stamped on reverse ricasso)

A very different style of presentation sword is exemplified by this piece given to General Grant by the Army of the Tennessee. The Bailey swords are quite ornate with engraved design and a literal use of enamel as a background to highlight certain decorative elements. The pieces made for Schuyler, Hartley and Graham (a retailing firm without manufacturing capacity), are highly figural with sculptural elements forming functional parts of the sword itself. This type of sword is illustrated in the Schuyler Hartley & Graham catalog of 1864 reprinted by Flayderman & Company in 1961.

Courtesy War Library and Museum MOLLUS

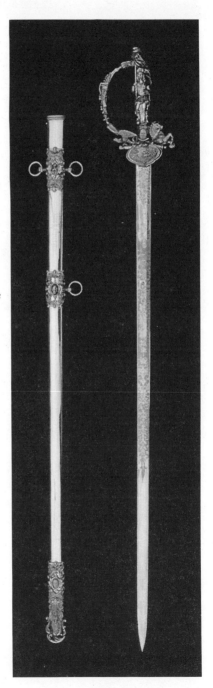

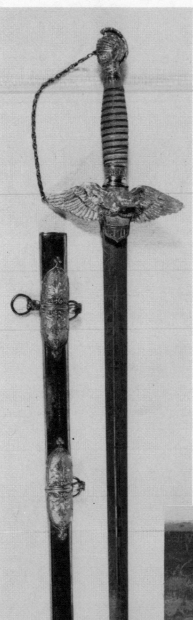

ARMY PRESENTATION SWORD TO GENERAL ALEXANDER SCHIMMELFENNIG 1863

Inscription: Presented to/ Gen. A Schimmelfennig/ by his staff/ 1863 (in script between the ring mounts of the scabbard).

Marks: none

Alexander Schimmelfennig was a Prussian officer who settled in Philadelphia in 1853. When hostilities broke out, Schimmelfennig became Colonel of the 74th Pennsylvania Volunteer Infantry. He was promoted to Brigadier General at the time of the second "Battle of Bull Run" and commanded a brigade of the XI Corps at Chancellorsville and Gettysburg. He was out of active participation in the war for some time because of malaria but was in command of the city of Charleston in 1865. He died of tuberculosis shortly thereafter in sick leave in Pennsylvania.

Courtesy; Pennsylvania Historical and Museum Commission 28.6.1

PRESENTATION SABER TO HUGH JUDSON KILPATRICK

Inscription: (On ring mount of the scabbard) To / Col. Judson Kilpatrick / from the / Officers & / of the / Harris Light Cavalry; (On lower ring mount) HLC.   Marks: (on ricasso-lightly stamped) (C?) Hors(?)er/ Solingen — This presumably refers to a member of the Horster family of bladesmiths who worked in Solingen during the nineteenth century.

Originally from New Jersey, Hugh Judson Kilpatrick was commissioned captain in the 5th New York Infantry in May, 1861. A few months later he was Lieutenant Colonel of the 2nd New York Cavalry, the Harris Light Cavalry from whom Kilpatrick obtained this saber. By December, 1862 Kilpatrick was Colonel of this unit and by June, 1863 he was in command of a cavalry brigade and ultimately a division taking part in virtually every cavalry action fought by the Army of the Potomac in 1863. He was later sent to join General Sherman in Georgia and participated in the "March to the Sea". He resigned from the Army in late 1865 to become minister to Chile. While little is known concerning the background of this saber, the fact that the saber's inscription addresses Kilpatrick as 'Col.' should date the piece to the interval between December, 1862, and his brigadier generalship the following June.   *Courtesy: Military History Research Collection, Carlisle Barracks, Pennsylvania*

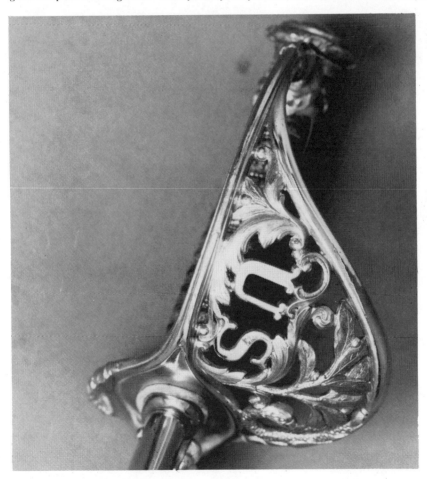

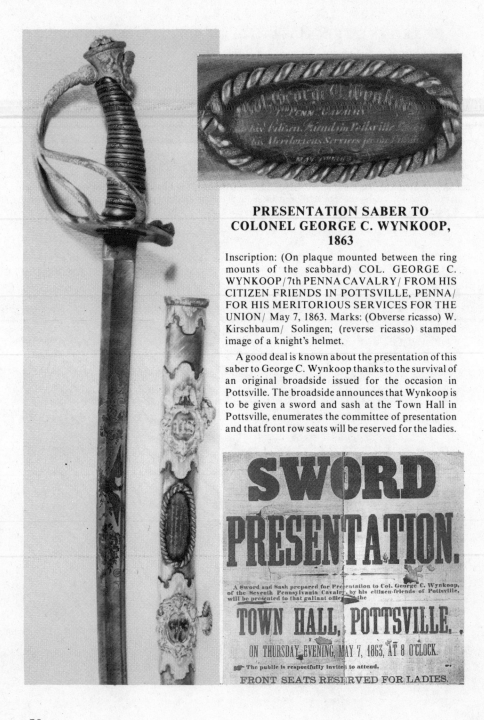

PRESENTATION SABER TO COLONEL GEORGE C. WYNKOOP, 1863

Inscription: (On plaque mounted between the ring mounts of the scabbard) COL. GEORGE C. WYNKOOP/7th PENNA CAVALRY/ FROM HIS CITIZEN FRIENDS IN POTTSVILLE, PENNA/ FOR HIS MERITORIOUS SERVICES FOR THE UNION/ May 7, 1863. Marks: (Obverse ricasso) W. Kirschbaum/ Solingen; (reverse ricasso) stamped image of a knight's helmet.

A good deal is known about the presentation of this saber to George C. Wynkoop thanks to the survival of an original broadside issued for the occasion in Pottsville. The broadside announces that Wynkoop is to be given a sword and sash at the Town Hall in Pottsville, enumerates the committee of presentation and that front row seats will be reserved for the ladies.

SWORD PRESENTATION.

A Sword and Sash prepared for Presentation to Col. George C. Wynkoop, of the Seventh Pennsylvania Cavalry, by his citizen-friends of Pottsville, will be presented to that gallant officer in the

TOWN HALL, POTTSVILLE,

ON THURSDAY EVENING, MAY 7, 1863, AT 8 O'CLOCK.

☞ The public is respectfully invited to attend.

FRONT SEATS RESERVED FOR LADIES.

That the presentation was accompanied by suitable speeches is noted in Wynkoop's biography.*

Wynkoop was a prominent figure in the Pennsylvania militia before the Civil War and came from a family noted for its military service. He was made one of four Brigadier Generals commanding Pennsylvania's initial three month volunteers. When the Seventh Pennsylvania Cavalry was formed as a three year unit in August, 1862, Wynkoop was given command of this regiment as its Colonel. The 7th was active in many of the engagements fought in Tennessee during the next year but Wynkoop was discharged on a surgeon's certificate in June, 1863. As the presentation date of the saber is in early May, Wynkoop must have returned to Pennsylvania during the Spring of 1863 —though not before participating in the hard fought engagements at Stone River and Gallatin, Tennessee. Wynkoop's eldest son was killed in the latter battle.

The saber is conspicuous for its use of diamond chips to form the letter 'W' in the scabbard and seed pearls which spell 'US'.   *Courtesy: Pennsylvania Historical and Museum Commission 52.10*

*Manuscript biography prepared by Ruth Paxon John of Downingtown, Pa. This document accompanied the sword and broadside to the PHMC collections in 1952.

SABER PRESENTED TO CAPTAIN C. C. McCORMICK, 1862

Inscription: (at throat of scabbard) Presented to/ CAPT. C C McCORMICK/ CO L, 7th PA. CAVALRY/ BY THE MEMBERS OF HIS COMPANY/ APRIL 6th 1863. Marks: H. Sauerbier Newark N J (etched on reverse of the ricasso).

Another presentation saber to an officer of the 7th Pennsylvania Cavalry is found in this saber to Charles C. McCormick, who, like Wynkoop, ultimately became Colonel of the regiment. Unlike Wynkoop who began his Civil War career as a Brigadier General, McCormick enlisted as a private in

Company D of the 7th. However, one month later he was elected Captain of Company L —the unit which gave him the present saber. In January, 1865, McCormick became Colonel of the regiment and was breveted a Brigadier General the following March. After the war McCormick served as a Major General in the National Guard of Pennsylvania. McCormick participated in the battles of Murfeesboro, Stone River, Chickamauga, Atlanta and Kenesaw Mountain and was twice wounded.

The McCormick saber was given to the PHMC in 1931 along with McCormick's spur, commissions, diaries and manuscript letters. One letter, dated May 12, 1863, and addressed to his sister by McCormick, describes the presentation of his saber: "About three days ago I took a pleasure ride out to our regiment, and about dark I was sitting in Col. Sipes' tent enjoying a glass of 'Ale' and a cigar when I was told that I was wanted at my old Company quarters. When I arrived there I found my Company drawn up in line in front of the Co. Hd. Quarters and all the officers of the regiment present. Just as I arrived in front of them a Sergeant stepped forward and in a beautiful little speech presented to me in behalf of the Company, an elegant Sword, Sword knot, Sash and Belt. I made them a little speech, and when I was through, they called for Bob, and presented him with one."

McCormick's "elegant sword" is dated April 6 in the presentation inscription on the scabbard. Evidently, McCormick, whose duty at the time was away from his regiment, was given the saber at the first opportunity. The scabbard is set with mother of pearl inlays.

Courtesy: Pennsylvania Historical and Museum Commission 31.46

PRESENTATION SABER TO COLONEL J. ARD MATHEWS 1863

Inscription: (on the faible of the blade etched) Presented to Colonel Joseph A. Mathews / from the Enlisted Men of the 128th Regt P.V./Stafford Court House, Va March 15, 1863. (On reverse faible of the blade) Manufactured by H Sauerbier Newark, N.J.

This second Sauerbier marked sword has many details reminiscent of the McCormick saber cited above. The general casting work is quite similar on the guard as is the overall style and curvature of the piece. The use of mother of pearl on the insets of the McCormick scabbard is similar to its use as the material of the grips on the Mathews piece. However, the Mathews saber is of extremely high quality while that given to McCormick is not of this grade. The grips and scabbard are of silver, either solid or extremely heavy plate. The saber is distinguished by a tintype of Mathews mounted in the pommel under glass. Also distinctive is a belt of woven silver embroidery which accompanied the sword.

Joseph Ard Mathews began his Civil War career as a Major of the 46th Pennsylvania (see page 66) in September, 1861. He was Colonel of the 128th Pennsylvania Volunteer Infantry on November 1, 1862. Less than two months after he received his presentation saber in March, Colonel Mathews and 225 of his men were captured at Chancellorsville. They were released by the Confederates because they had only a short time before their nine month enlistments would expire. A year later Mathews was Colonel of the 205th Pennsylvania Volunteer Infantry and was Brevetted Brigadier General in April, 1865. He was mustered out two months later on June 2, 1865.

Along with this saber, which is in the Commonwealth's collections, the Mifflin County Historical Society has a presentation saddle given to Mathews at the same time as this saber by the Enlisted Men of the 128th P.V.I.
Courtesy: Pennsylvania Historical and Museum Commission 27.24

53

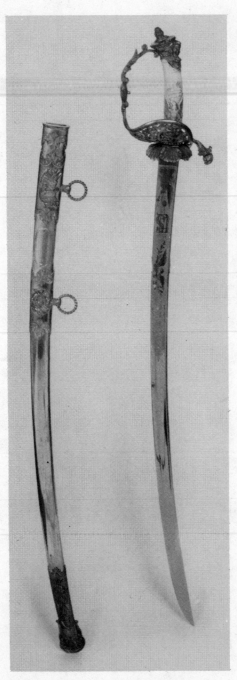

PRESENTATION SABER TO LT COL GABRIEL MIDDLETON

Inscription: (engraved on silver plaque between the ring mounts) Lt. Col. G. Middleton/ presented by the officers of the/ 20th Penna. Cav. A testimonial of/ merit as a gallant, efficient, and/ gentlemanly officer.

Marks: W Clauberg/ Solingen (in two lines stamped on reverse ricasso).

This unusual presentation saber is very similar in hilt design to the Bean sword (see page 70) which was sold by G.W. Simons of Philadelphia.

Middleton began his Civil War career as a Captain of Company E , 2nd Pennsylvania Cavalry. He later served as a Lieutenant Colonel of the 20th Pennsylvania Cavalry and as Colonel of the regiment from January through June 1865. The undated presentation saber must have been given to Middleton between his promotion to Lieutenant Colonel (February 22, 1864) and his promotion to Colonel on January 15, 1865. The regiment served with distinction in the Shenendoah Valley area and in West Virginia. *Courtesy: War Library and Museum MOLLUS*

PRESENTATION SWORD TO GENERAL HECTOR TYNDALE

Inscription: (engraved between the ring mounts of the scabbard) Presented to Genl. Hector Tyndale/ by J. Mc. L.

Marks C.R. Kirschbaum/ Solingen (die stamped on the obverse ricasso).

While we do not know the circumstances behind the presentation of this sword, its general configuration is highly reminiscent of a 17th century broadsword rather than the US Army patterns of the time. It has a German silver scabbard and a straight blade with an elongated single fuller.

General Tyndale was a Philadelphia native and an authority on ceramics. He attended John Brown on the scaffold and escorted his body for burial. He was commissioned Major in the 28th Pennsylvania Volunteer Infantry in June 1861. He was promoted to Brigadier General in April, 1863, and served with the XI Corps. He resigned because of illness in August, 1864, but was brevetted Major General the following March in recognition of his past services.

Courtesy: War Library and Museum MOLLUS

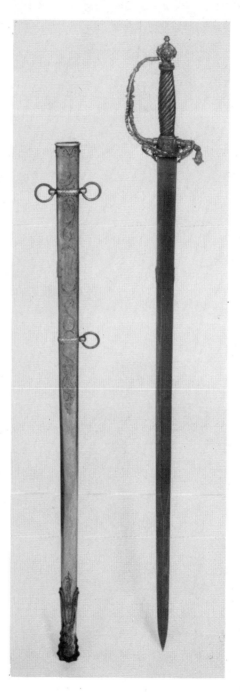

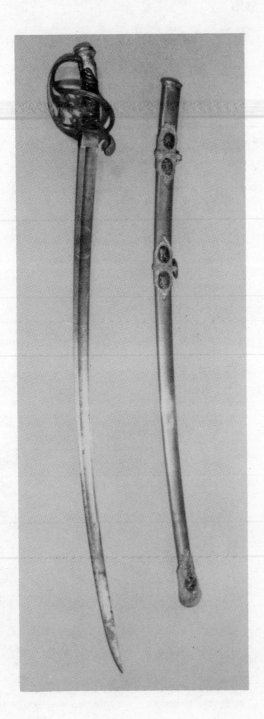

PRESENTATION SABER TO COL. THOMAS E. ROSE, 1863

Inscription: (engraved on scabbard between the ring mounts) Presented to/ Col. Thos. Ellewood Rose/by/the Officers of the 77th Regt. Pa. Vols as a token of respect for their/ Gallant Leader/ A.D. 1863. Marks: stamped SOLINGEN on the obverse ricasso; Schuyler, Hartley/&/Graham/ N.Y. (etched below ricasso).

The Rose saber is similar to the McCormick and Mathews sabers cited above. All three may have gone thru the hands of Schuyler, Hartley & Graham. Henry Sauerbier, described in both the Newark city directories and the R.G. Dun ratings as a tool manufacturer and a cutler, probably did not actually market the swords which bear his name. He certainly did manufacture blades end evidently etched them as well. It is possible to speculate that he made the other parts of his swords as well, though in the case of the Rose saber, the blade is marked Solingen. At the same time, the details of the hilts and scabbards are sufficiently similar that it is possible to say that the Sauerbier marked McCormick saber and the Schuyler, Hartley and Graham marked Rose saber came from the same hand.

Thomas E. Rose was mustered in as Captain of Company B, 77th Pennsylvania Volunteer Infantry. He was promoted to Colonel of the regiment in January of 1863, and was captured at Chickamauga in September of that year. Exchanged the following June, he commanded the 1st Brigade of the 1st Division, 4th Army Corps. The most famous episode of Colonel Rose's career was his escape from Libby Prison in February, 1864. Rose and 105 Union officers tunnelled their way to freedom from a store room in the prison. Rose remained in the Army as a captain after the war and retired as a major in 1894. *Courtesy: Mercer Museum 19492*

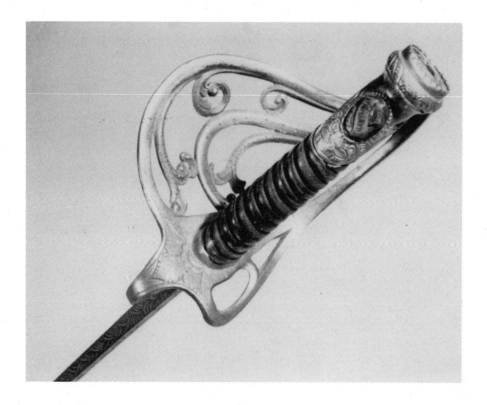

PRESENTATION SWORD TO MAJOR J.K. BOLTON, 1865

Inscription: (engraved on plaque mounted between ring mounts) Presented to Major J K Bolton /51st Regt Pa, Vet: Vol: by the members,/ of Co: A as a token of respect/ NORRISTOWN Pa March 5th 1865. Marks: W H Horstmann & Sons Philadelphia (in circle on obverse ricasso); Clauberg/Solingen (on reverse ricasso); Iron Proof (on quill)

Joseph K. Bolton was mustered in as a captain in the 51st Pennsylvania Volunteer Infantry in August, 1861, and served with that regiment throughout the war. His promotion to Major in January, 1865, is reflected in this sword's presentation the following March. The sword features the extremely high quality etched blades known to have been imported by Horstmann during the Civil War. The scabbard is of the typical Horstmann style with silver ovals inserted in the tang mounts of the scabbard. One of the ovals is engraved with an eagle, wings spread and the other a seated Columbia.

Courtesy: Pennsylvania Historical and Museum Commission 6.18

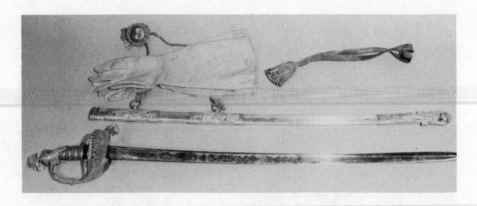

SWORD PRESENTED TO LT. COLONEL ROBERT BODINE, 1864

Inscription: Presented to/ Lt. Col. Robt. L. Bodine/ by the Veterans of the 26th Reg Pa. Vols/ for his brave and gallant conduct in the field/ and regard for him as an officer & Gentleman/ April lst 1864. (Engraved on scabbard).

Marks: Grey 627/Arch (St)/Philad (On obverse ricasso); Warranted to Cut Wrought Iron (Etched on blade)

Robert L. Bodine began his career as a Commissary Sergeant in the 26th Pennsylvania Volunteer Infantry in 1861. Two months later he was a Lieutenant and advanced through each rank to that of Lieutenant Colonel in October, 1863. While Bodine was mustered out in June, 1864, he was later brevetted Colonel and Brigadier General in March, 1865, for his previous conduct. The date of the presentation of this sword, April 1, 1864, probably reflects the occasion of his actual retirement.

This staff and field officer's sword was presented to the Bucks County Historical Society by Bodine's grandson and includes a presentation case, gloves and sword knot. The maker of the hilt and scabbard was, in all probability, William H Gray. Gray emerges from a number of other persons of the same name in the Philadelphia directories as a silverplater in 1845. He advertises as a maker of military ornaments in 1856, and as an epaulette manufacturer in 1862. His 1863 listing is as a sword manufacturer and continues through 1865. Gray turned to the kindred manufacture of gas fixtures after the Civil War.

Courtesy: Mercer Museum 26491

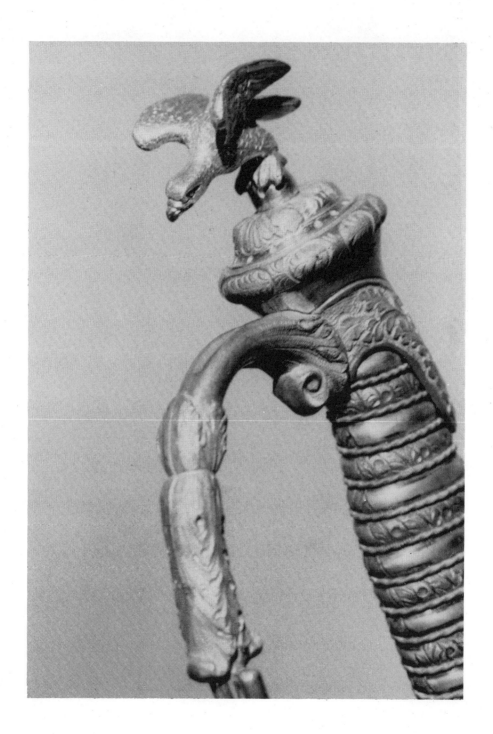

MODEL 1850 STAFF AND FIELD OFFICERS' SWORD PRESENTED TO ANDREW H. TIPPIN

Inscription: Presented to/ Col. Andrw H. Tippin/ by the Non Comd Officers & Privates of the 68th Regt. Pa. Vols. (Engraved on scabbard)

Marks: Gray/ 627 Arch/ Philada (on obverse ricasso): W Clauberg (on reverse ricasso)

Colonel Tippin was mustered as colonel of the 68th Pennsylvania Volunteer Infantry in June, 1862, and served with the regiment's three year term thru June of 1865. He had previously served as a Lieutenant in the Mexican War. At the outbreak of the Civil War he became Colonel of the three month 20th Pennsylvania Volunteer Infantry.

This Gray presentation sword is very similar to the Bodine sword cited above. The additional mark on the blade of W Clauberg indicates that Gary, as a silverplater and brass caster was not capable of manufacturing sword blades, indeed very few firms were so equipped, and obtained his blades elsewhere, in this case from Solingen. *Courtesy: Pottstown Historical Society*

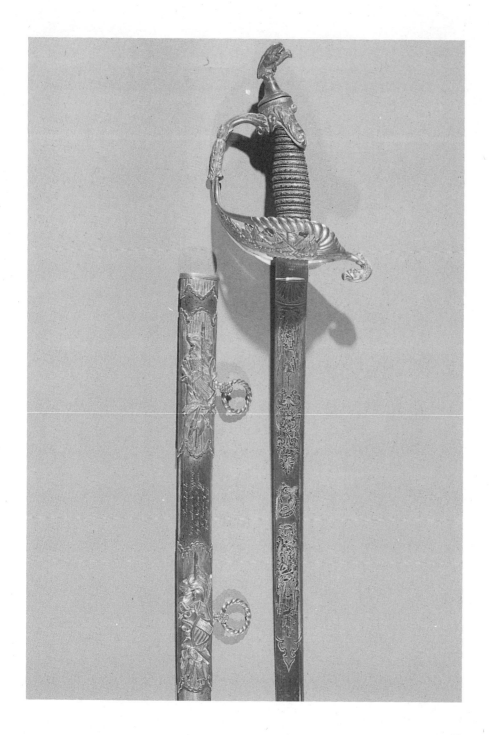

PRESENTATION SWORD TO COLONEL HUGH McNEIL, 1862

Inscription: TO/ COL HUGH/W McNEIL/ 1st PENN RIFLES (BUCKTAILS)/ CAMP PIERPONT, VA/ FEB 18, 1862 (on reverse of scabbard at upper ring mount BY CO D THE RAFTSMAN GUARDS (engraved deer head) (inscribed on sword guard).

Marks: COLLINS & CO / HARTFORD CT (on reverse ricasso); Tiffany & Co (engraved on reverse forte of the blade); TIFFANY & CO (above legend on ring mount bearing presentation inscription)

This important sword was given to the Colonel of a well known Pennsylvania regiment, the Bucktails, by D Company, composed of men whose civilian livlihood were raftsmen on Pennsylvania's rivers. Hugh McNeil, a lawyer and Yale graduate was captain of this company of the 42nd Pennsylvania Volunteer Infantry. Less than one month after the February, 1862, presentation of this sword, McNeil stated in a letter to his sister that his new sword was the "...finest thing I ever saw. Too nice for ordinary wear." He went on to relate that he had left the sword in Washington and that his family should retrieve it if McNeil were killed. This prophecy proved all too true as Colonel Hugh McNeil did not survive the Battle of Antietam in September of that year. Evidently, the family did pick up the sword as it was given by them to the Commonwealth in 1960.

Courtesy: Pennsylvania Historical and Museum Commission 60.19

MODEL 1850 STAFF AND FIELD OFFICERS' SWORD PRESENTED TO MAJOR JOSEPH A. MATHEWS, 1862

Inscription: Presented to/ MAJOR J. ARD MATTHEWS (sic)/ of the 46th Regt. P.V. / by the Citizens of/ MIFFLIN CO Pa/ Sept 1862 (on brass plaque between mounts). Marks: G.W. SIMONS & BRO (etched on obverse ricasso)

Major Mathews is the same person as the Colonel Mathews of the 128th Pennsylvania Volunteer Infantry who received the magnificent silver mounted saber described on page 53. Mathews first served with the 46th P.V.I. before becoming Colonel of the 128th P.V.I.

Courtesy: Mifflin County Historical Society

Note: Also in the Mifflin County Historical Society's collections is a presentation saddle to Mathews from the Enlisted Men of the 128th P.V.I. dated at the same time as the silver presentation sword and belt in the PHMC collections.

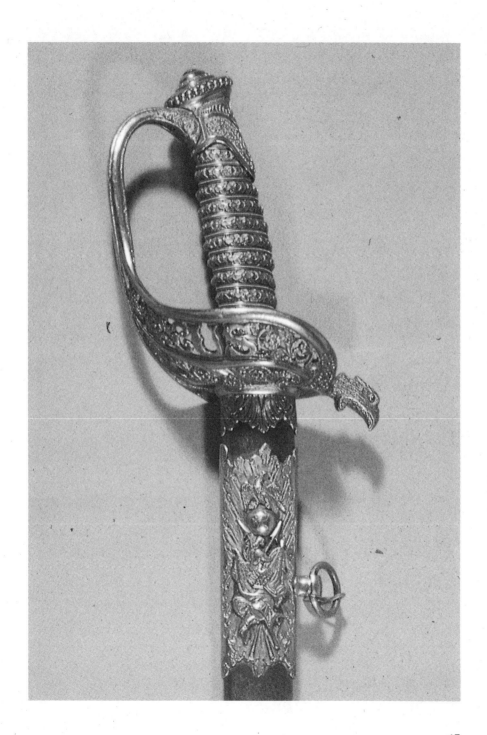

MODEL 1850 STAFF AND FIELD OFFICERS SWORD PRESENTED TO HENRY PLEASANTS, 1862

Inscription: Presented by the / TOWER GUARDS/ Comp'y C 48th Regt Penn,Vol./ to their/ Captain Henry Pleasants/ at New Bern NC 1862; Marks: W.H./ Horstmann/ & Sons/ Philadelphia (etched on obverse ricasso); Iron Proof (etched on reverse ricasso)

General Pleasants, best known for his mining of the "Crater" at Petersburg, was a railroad engineer with the Pennsylvania Railroad and a practicing mine engineer as well. In September, 1861, he became Captain of Company C, 48th Pennsylvania Volunteer Infantry and was promoted to Lieutenant Colonel in September, 1862. He was mustered out when his term expired in December, 1864, but was brevetted Brigadier General in 1865. He returned to Pennsylvania after the war and became Chief Engineer with the Philadelphia and Reading Coal Company. *Courtesy: Pennsylvania Historical and Museum Commission 34.2.1*

MODEL 1850 STAFF AND FIELD OFFICERS' SWORD PRESENTED TO COL. GEORGE P. McLEAN, 1862

Inscription: Presented to COL. GEO. P. McLEAN/Commanding 88 Regt. Penna. Vols /By the Loyal Citizens of Alexandria Va/ for the efficient manner in which he/ has sustained the cause of the UNION/ while quartering among us/ February 22, 1862. Marks : Marked IRON PROOF on ricasso

George P. McLean was mustered in as Major of the three month 22nd P.V.I. in April of 1861. Shortly after the term of this regiment expired he became Colonel of the 88th P.V.I. at Washington in which he served for the next fourteen months, resigning in December, 1862. He also served in the emergency militia raised in 1863 as Colonel of the 59th Regiment.

Courtesy: The Union League

MODEL 1850 STAFF AND FIELD OFFICERS SWORD PRESENTED TO LIEUTENANT ISAAC SEESHOLTZ

Inscription: Presented to/ lst Lieutenant Isaac H. Seesholtz/ Compy E, 118th Regt. Penna. Vols./ by his friends/ the Old Members of Compy. C/ as a testimonial of their regard.

Marks: Mintzer/ Philadelphia (stamped on reverse of ricasso); Beehive stamp on obverse ricasso

Isaac H. Seesholtz of Catawissa, Pa, was a medical student at the outbreak of the Civil War. He enrolled in April, 1861 in the 6th Pennsylvania Reserve and was mustered in as a 2nd Lieutenant. He resigned in October and enlisted as a Sergeant in Company H, 99th P.V.I. He was promoted to 2nd Lieutenant early in 1862 and as a lst Lieutenant in May. He was discharged the next month and later served with the 118th Pennsylvania Volunteer Infantry.

William Mintzer was a military goods dealer in Philadelphia from well before the Civil War until his death in 1869. *Courtesy: War Library and Museum MOLLUS*

Opposite:

MODEL 1850 STAFF AND FIELD OFFICERS' SWORD PRESENTED TO CAPTAIN B.F. BEAN

Inscription: Presented to/ CAPT. BENJ. F. BEAN. by members of. CO B. 34th REG. P.V as a token of regard for his soldierly/qualities and gentlemanly /conduct (engraved on a silver plaque between the ring mounts); "CAPT. B.F. BEAN" (etched on the obverse of the blade). Marks: G.W. Simons./ & Bro. / Philada, Pa. (etched on obverse ricasso). Unknown bladesmith's geometrical mark on obverse ricasso.

Benjamin F. Bean was mustered in as a Captain of Company I, 129th Pennsylvania Volunteer Infantry but was mustered out the following May. His next service was as Captain of Company B 34th Infantry in the 1863 Pennsylvania Militia raised at the time of the Confederate invasion which culminated with the Battle of Gettysburg. Presumably, the sword dates to this brief period.

The sword is a high quality Simons piece (see pages 67 and 77 for other Simons swords) distinguished by the eagle finial on the guard with small ruby chips in its eyes. The present sword has an added counter guard which extends over the throat of the scabbard in the shape of a leaf. The sword is gilt with silver grips and one German silver ring mount. *Courtesy: The Union League 79.1.3*

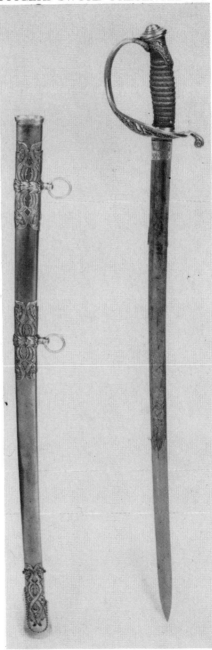

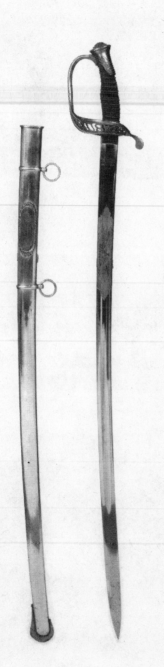

MODEL 1850 STAFF AND FIELD OFFICERS SWORD PRESENTED TO SAMUEL T. DAVIS, 1863

Inscription: To Adjt. Sam'l T. Davis/ 77th Regt. P.V.s by his friends in/ Ohavers Creek Valley, Pa as a token of/ their appreciation of his gallant service/ in behalf of his country, Nov'r. 1863 (engraved on a brass plaque between the scabbard ring mounts); Shiloh/ Corinth/ Lavergne/ Tricene/ Stone River/ Liberty Gap/ & Chicamaugua (plaque on reverse of scabbard). Marks: W.H./ Horstmann/& Sons/ Philadelphia (etched on obverse ricasso); Crowned head stamped on blade at reverse ricasso.

Samuel T. Davis enrolled at Petersburg, Pa. in August, 1861, and became a 2nd Lieutenant of Company G, 77th Pennsylvania Volunteer Infantry. He was promoted to lst Lieutenant and Adjutant in September, 1861, and to Captain in December, 1863. He was wounded at Resaca, Georgia, in May of 1864, and was discharged on a surgeon's certificate the following August.

MODEL 1850 STAFF AND FIELD OFFICERS SWORD PRESENTED TO COL. PETER ELLMAKER, 1862

Inscription: Col PETER C. ELLMAKER/ 1st Regiment(Gray Reserves)/Reserve Brigade 1st Division/ Pennsylvania Volunteers from/ THE REGIMENT JANUARY 1st 1862 (engraved on an oval plaque mounted between the ring mounts of the scabbard). Marks: W.H. Horstmann & Sons/ Philadelphia (etched on ricasso)

Colonel Ellmaker commanded the Gray Reserves from April 1861 through August, 1862. In September of that year he became Colonel of the 119th Pennsylvania Volunteer Infantry and served through December, 1864, when he was discharged. *Courtesy: 1st Regiment Infantry Museum*

MODEL 1850 FOOT OFFICERS SWORD
PRESENTED TO
COLONEL THOMAS A. ROWLEY,
1862

Inscription: Presented to/Col. Thos A. Rowley/ by the Officers of the /13th Regt. Pa Vols./ Jany 25th 1862 (engraved on scabbard between the ring mounts). Marks: Ames Mfg Co/Chicopee/ Mass (etched on obverse ricasso); Made by/ Ames Mfg Co/ Chicopee Mass (stamped into reverse of scabbard)

Thomas A. Rowley was mustered in as Colonel of the three month 13th Pennsylvania Volunteer Infantry. After their term expired he became Colonel of the 102nd P.V.I. in August and was wounded at Fair Oaks. He was appointed Brigadier General in November, 1862, and commanded the 3rd Brigade of the 3rd Division, VI Corps at Fredericksburg. He also commanded a brigade in this Army Corps at Gettysburg. However, Rowley was court martialed in April, 1864. While ultimately restored to duty, he resigned in December of that year.

The Rowley sword was received with his gloves, spurs and sash. It also has a surviving field scabbard of gilt brass and leather in addition to the all brass presentation scabbard. This scabbard is also marked by the Ames Mfg. Co

Courtesy: Pennsylvania Historical and Museum Commission 34.122

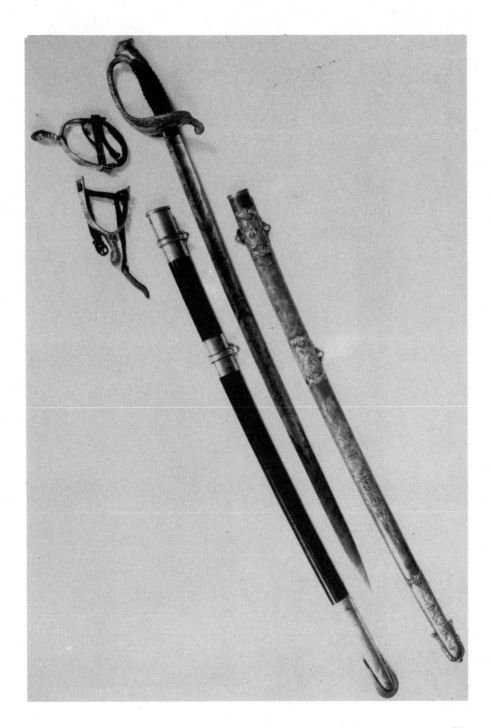

MODEL 1850 STAFF AND FIELD OFFICERS SWORD PRESENTED TO CAPTAIN A.W. DECKER

Inscription: To/ CAPT. A.W. DECKER/CO. K, 202 Reg . Pa. Vols/ from/ his command/ Oct. 4, 1864/ COM. ON PURCHASE/ & PRESENTATION/ Lieut. J.S. Morrison P. Shaver/ Sergt H. Hudson/ D.R. Belts/ Chapln A B Miller (engraved on German silver scabbard on reverse near throat). Marks: W/ Clauberg/ Solingen (on reverse ricasso)

Andrew W. Decker was mustered in as Captain of Company K 202nd Pennsylvania Volunteer Infantry in September, 1864, from Northumberland County. He was mustered out in August, 1865.

Decker's sword is highly unusual with ivory grips having the relief figure of a curirass with crossed rammers beneath a German silver plated scabbard with brass fittings and a blade etched ONWARD TO VICTORY

Courtesy: Pennsylvania Historical and Museum Commission 70.93.1

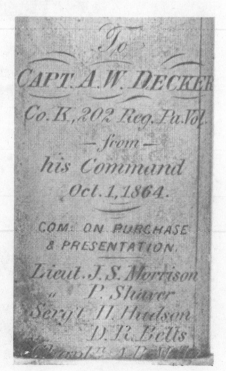

MODEL 1850 STAFF AND FIELD OFFICERS SWORD PRESENTED TO CAPTAIN WILLIAM E. SEES

Inscription: Presented to/ Capt. W.E. Sees/ Co. D llth Reg. P.V./ as a token of respect/D.J. Unger/P. Linn/E.P. Hachuten/ B.F. Chandler/W.P. Hachuten/ B.G. Peters. Marks: G.W. Simons & Bro/in Philadelphia (etched on both sides of blade on ricasso) IRON: PROOF (on quill).

William E. Sees was mustered in as Captain of Company D, llth Pennsylvania Volunteer Infantry and mustered out September 25, 1862. He was from Lycoming County, Pennsylvania. With his sword, a sword belt and sash were donated to the Commonwealth in 1960 by Sees' grandson.

Courtesy: Pennsylvania Historical and Museum Commission 60.12

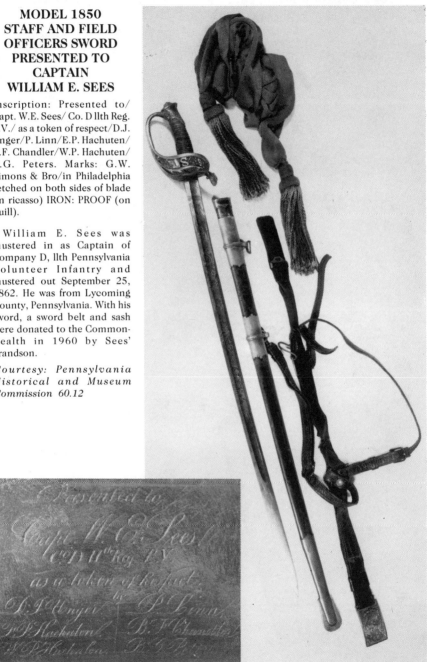

MODEL 1850 FOOT OFFICERS SWORD PRESENTED TO
CAPTAIN J. ROSS CLARK, 1861

Inscription: Presented to/ CAPTAIN J. ROSS CLARK./ Company D, Gray Reserves, as a token of esteem/ BY THE MEMBERS OF THE CORPS./ Philada. July 23d. 1861 (plaque mounted on sharkskin scabbard between the ring mounts). Marks: none

J. Ross Clark is first listed on the militia records of the state during the 1862 emergency in which the Gray Reserves was called. He later served in the 1863 emergency call up of Pennsylvania militia in 1863.

Courtesy: 1st Regiment Museum.

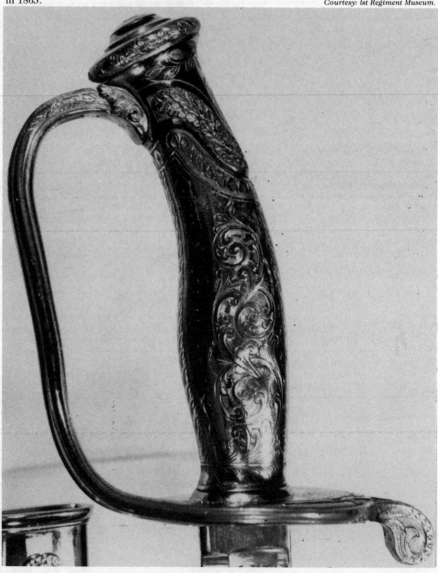

SWORD PRESENTED TO CAPTAIN POINSETT COOPER

Inscription: Presented to/ Captain Poinsett Cooper/ by the President, Directors, and Officers/ of the Brooklyn Bank (engraved on the scabbard between the ring mounts) Balls Bluff, Seven Pines, Fair Oaks, Gaines Mills, Malvern Hill, 2nd Bull Run, Antietam, Fredericksburgh, Bristow Station, Gettysburgh, Wilderness (on bottom portion of scabbard).

Marks: Clauberg/ Solingen (stamped on reverse of ricasso). In case with Schuyler, Hartley and Graham label.

This sword is very reminiscent of French pieces of the era. Considering Schuyler, Hartley and Graham's import trade — Marcellus Hartley was in Europe purchasing arms for the Federal government — it is entirely possible that the sword itself is French. Poinsett Cooper was Captain in the 42nd New York Volunteer Infantry.

Courtesy: War Library and Museum, MOLLUS

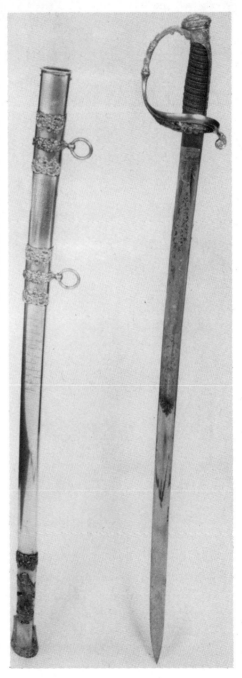

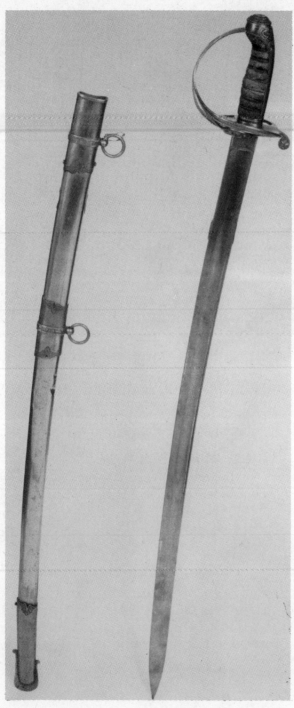

PRESENTATION SECONDARY MARTIAL SWORD TO CAPTAIN JOHN LOCKHART, 1863

Inscription: Presented to/ Capt. John Lockhart/ by the Employees of/ Messrs Krider & Biddle/ May 1, 1863 (on top ring mount); John Lockhard (sic) rev. of blade. Marks: C.R. Kirschbaum/ Solingen stamped into obverse ricasso.

John Lockhart served as 1st Lieutenant, Captain and Major with the 72nd Pennsylvania Volunteer Infantry (Baxter Fire Zouaves). His three year enrollment ended in August of 1864, and he was discharged shortly after attaining the rank of major in July, 1864. *Courtesy: War Library and Museum, MOLLUS*

SABER PRESENTED TO CAPTAIN LEWIS MERRILL, 1861

Inscription: Capt. Lewis Merrill/2nd Dragoons/ USA (on brass scabbard between the ring mounts) The officers of the 1st Regt Nebraska/Volunteers to Capt. Lewis Merrill/ 2nd Dragoons USA August 1861 (etched on obverse of blade) The Constitution and Union Forever (on the reverse of the blade).
Marks: none

Lewis Merrill was a regular Army officer from Pennsylvania. He graduated the Military Academy in 1851 and served with the US Dragoons through the remainder of the 1850's. He became Colonel of the 2nd Missouri Cavalry in August, 1861, and served with distinction in Missouri, Arkansas and Georgia. Merrill stayed in the Army after the War and was brevetted Brigadier General in 1890 for an action against the Indians some thirteen years earlier. He had already been brevetted Brigadier General during the Civil War but, like all officers who elected to continue their service, reverted to his permanent rank after the conclusion of hostilities.

Courtesy: War Library and Museum MOLLUS

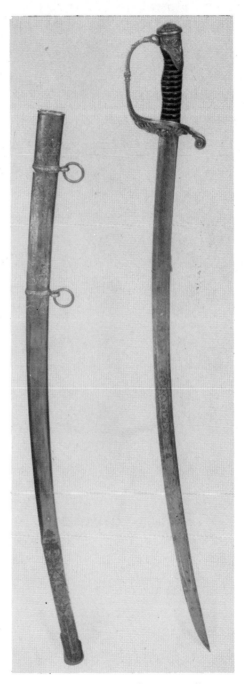

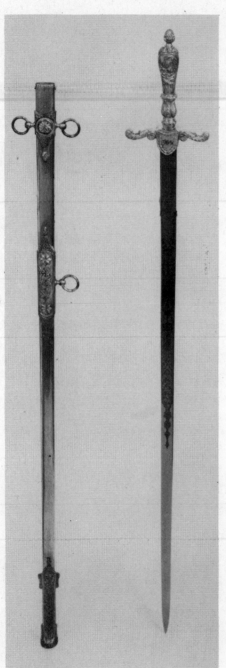

MODEL 1840 MEDICAL STAFF SWORD OF PAUL BECK GODDARD

Inscription: PBG in blue enamel on obverse langet.

Marks: Bailey & Co/ Philada (on obverse ricasso of blade etched)

This unusual Medical staff sword was made by the jewelry producing firm of Bailey & Co. The dates and circumstances of the sword's coming to Goddard are unknown. He was a surgeon with the Pennsylvania Volunteers as of October 4, 1862, and was discharged April 8, 1865, but died the following year. He is mentioned in Taylor, *Philadelphia in the Civil War*, as surgeon in charge of the Master Street Hospital.

Courtesy: War Library and Museum, MOLLUS

PRESENTATION SWORD TO CAPTAIN HENRY STELLWAGON BY THE BRITISH GOVERNMENT 1864

Inscription:
PRESENTED BY THE BRITISH GOVERNMENT / TO CAPTAIN HENRY S. STELLWAGON OF THE NAVY OF THE UNITED STATES OF AMERICA / IN GRATEFUL ACKNOWLEDGEMENT OF SERVICES TO THE CREW OF THE BRITISH BRIGANTINE 'MERSEY' 1864. (On obverse of Marks: Charles Smith & Sons / 12 Piccadilly / London (etched on obverse ricasso).

Stellwagon is listed in the Navy Register of 1865 as Captain of the USS Constellation.   *Courtesy: Historical Society of Pennsylvania*

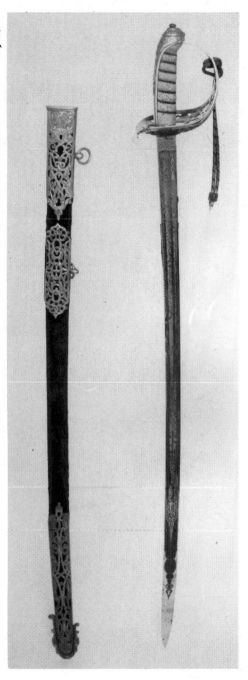

Opposite page:

MODEL 1860 STAFF OFFICERS SWORD PRESENTED TO CAPTAIN THEO. WIEDERSHEIM

Inscription: Presented to/ CAPT. THEO. E WIEDERSHEIM,/ Comd'g D. Co, First Reg. Infty. N.G.P./by MAJOR EDWIN N. BENSON./ Sept. 12th 1877. (engraved on brass plaque screwed to the scabbard). Marks: W.H. Horstmann/ & Sons/ Philadelphia (on obverse ricasso)

Theodore Wiedersheim enlisted in the Gray Reserves in August of 1862. He was promoted through the ranks to 2nd Lieutenant in November, 1873, and was Colonel of the Regiment by 1878. He resigned in May, 1887.   *Courtesy: lst Regiment Museum*

Right:

MODEL 1860 STAFF OFFICERS SWORD PRESENTED TO COLONEL J.P.F. GOBIN, 1884

Inscription: Presented to Col. J.P.F. Gobin 8th Regt N.G.P./ Officers and Enlisted Men of the Regiment/ As a token of their respect and esteem/ Camp Getty / Aug 7 1884. Marks: William H. Horstmann/ & Sons/ Philadelphia (on obverse ricasso)

J.P.S. Gobin was mustered as a lst Lieutenant in Company F of the llth Pennsylvania Volunteer Infantry in April, 1861. He served as a captain in the later (3 year) 47th P.V.I. and became colonel of that regiment in January, 1865. He was brevetted brigadier general in March of that year. Gobin continued his military career with the National Guard of Pennsylvania after the war becoming captain of the Coleman Guards in 1871 and colonel of the 8th Regiment in 1874. He was re-elected colonel in 1884 and appointed brigadier general in 1885. With the exception of his active duty role in the Spanish-American War, Gobin continued as a general officer in the National Guard of Pennsylvania thru 1907.

The present sword was donated by a descendent of a contemporary of Gobin's, Adjutant General Frank Beary, in 1966.

Courtesy: Pennsylvania Historical and Museum Commission 79.4

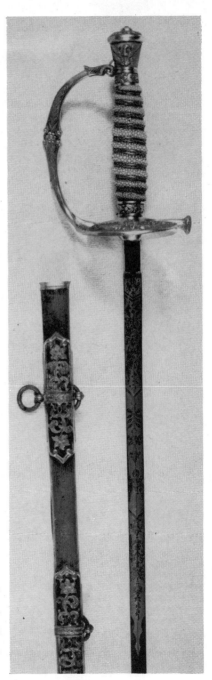

SWORD PRESENTED TO COLONEL HENRY L. CAKE BY THE 96th P.V.I.
1863

Description: Gilt hilt and scabbard with elaborate gilt etching on the blade. There is a shield of the United States mounted upon the solid guard and covered by blue hard paste enamel (possibly by F. Bailey & Company of Philadelphia). On the scabbard are two very well engraved battle scenes on the reverse and the Arms of Pennsylvania as well as a mounted horseman on the obverse. Between these two overlays is a cut out of Cake's initials in diamond chips. A similar overlay is mounted on the shield mounted on the sword guard. The blade is probably German and very well made as well as damascened. Etching in gold is also well done on the blade. The manufacturer's name is executed in silver wire by the ricasso. Blade 31¾", overall 39". Sword in scabbard 40".

Inscription: (on scabbard reverse between engravings — abbreviated) COL HENRY L. CAKE by the Officers and Soldiers of the 96th Regt. P.V. . . . . A lengthy inscription describes Cake's service at West Point (VA), Gaines Hill (Mill) and Charles City Cross Roads and his services both in the field and on the march.

Manufacturer: G.W./SIMONS & BRO/PHILADELPHIA in silver wire on the ricasso. The extreme quality of this piece and the use of hard paste enamel leads to the speculation that the sword was actually made by F. Bailey & Co. for Simons. Other hard paste enamel decorated swords are marked with the Bailey name.

  Cake was a newspaper publisher in Pottsville before the Civil War. During that conflict he commanded first the 25th P.V.I. and, from September 1861 through March 1863, the 96th P.V.I. In all probability the sword was given to Cake at the time of his retirement from that regiment on or about March 12, 1863. After the war, Cake sold anthracite mining machinery and served two terms in Congress — 1867-1871. Courtesy: Schuylkill County Historical Society 84.100

PRESENTATION SWORD TO
BREVET MAJOR GENERAL GALUSHA PENNYPACKER

Inscription: (block capital letters) "PRESENTED TO / BREVET MAJOR GENERAL /
G. PENNYPACKER / U.S. ARMY / BY HIS CHESTER COUNTY FRIENDS"

Maker's Mark: "V (?) Clauberg / Solingen"
Overall length: 40". Blade length: 32¾".

Sold by: "W.H. Horstmann / & Sons / Philadelphia"

Inscription on blade: "Union for ever"

Courtesy: Chester County Historical Society, West Chester, PA

PRESENTATION SWORD TO
CAPT. N. A. PENNYPACKER

Inscription: (script) "TESTIMONIAL / TO / CAPT N.A. PENNYPACKER / BY MEMBERS OF Co. K 4th REGIMENT / P.R.V.C. / NOVEMBER 21, 1863"

Maker's Mark: "W. Clauberg / Solingen". "Iron Proof" on flat edge of blade.

Overall length: 39¾". Blade length: 32".

Courtesy: Chester County Historical Society, West Chester, PA

MODEL 1850 STAFF AND FIELD OFFICERS SWORD PRESENTED TO COL. JOSEPH KNIPE

Inscription: Presented to Col Joseph F Knipe of/ the 46th . Reg Pa. Vol. for gallantry in/ Battles of Newtown, Middletown, Winchester,/ and Slaughters Mountain, by his friends/ Harrisburg, Septr 6th. 1862. Marks: 1861 (on obverse ricasso)

General Knipe was one of the first to volunteer his services in 1861 and was given command of the 46th Pennsylvania Volunteer Infantry in August, 1861. He was promoted to Brigadier General of US Volunteers in November of 1862 and served as a general officer through some of the hardest fought engagements of the war. He commanded the lst Brigade of the lst Division XII Corps which, redesignated as the XX Corps, participated in the Chatanooga and Atlanta campaigns. Knipe became Chief of Cavalry in the Army of the Tennessee and commanded the 7th Division Cavalry Corps, Military Division of the Mississippi. He was wounded at Cedar Mountain and Winchester. *Courtesy: Pennsylvania Historical and Museum Commission 61.30*

MODEL 1850 OFFICERS SWORD
PRESENTED TO
LIEUT. WILLIAM S. MOORHEAD

Inscription: Presented to Lieut Wm S. Moorhead by the Non Commissioned Officers and Privates of Co. K, 76th Regt P.V. as a Testimony of their Esteem for him as an Officer and Soldier (engraved silver presentation plaque on scabbard between ring mounts). Reverse of scabbard engraved with engagements and dates as follows:

> Fort Pulaski, Ga. April 10, 1862
> James Island June 14, 1862
> Pocotaglio, S.C. Oct. 22, 1862
> Morris Island June 10, 1863
> Fort Wagner, S.C. July 11, 1863
> Fort Wagner, S.C. July 13, 1863
> Drury's Bluff, Va. May 16, 1864
> Chapin's Farm
>   Fort Gilmer
> Fort Harrison Sept. 28, 1864
> Cold Harbor June 1-3, 1864
> Strawberry Plains
> Petersburg Heights, Va. Juny 30, 1864
> Mine Explosion
> Deep Bottom, Va. Aug. 16, 1864
> Darbytown Road, Va. Oct. 27, 1864
> Weldon Rail Road, Va. May 5,6 & 7, 1864
> Fort Fisher, N.C. Jan. 15, 1865

Marks: W. H. Horstmann & Sons over Philadelphia, struck with King's head proof (on obverse ricasso); Iron Proof (on reverse ricasso). Blade: etched with gilt outlined panels — eagle on obverse, US on reverse. Guard: U and S separated by fierce eagle attacking serpent. Pommel: perched eagle.

Overall length: 39½ inches; blade length 32¼ inches.

William S. Moorhead, a merchant in Philadelphia, enrolled on September 15, 1861, at the age of 20. He became 1st Sgt. on November 28, 1861; Pr. 2nd Lieut. on March 30, 1863; 1st Lieut. on July 25, 1864; and Captain on September 5, 1864. (Pr. Major, July 1, 1865 — not mustered.)

Courtesy: War Library and Museum MOLLUS

PRESENTATION SABER TO MAJOR JOHN E. WYNKOOP 7th PENNSYLVANIA CAVALRY 1863

Inscription: Presented by the Citizens of Pottsville/to/Major John Estelle Wynkoop/ 7th PA CAV/in appreciation of his military services at/MURFEESBORO, FRANKLIN, CHAPLAIN HILL & ELSEWHERE, 1863.

Maker: (etched at ricasso) G.W./SIMONS & BRO/PHILADA.

This is a cavalry saber with solid silver grip and a gilt hilt and scabbard. The presentation inscription is located on a silver plate mounted on the scabbard. Of the three scabbard ornaments, only the US with seed pearls remains. From a similar sword in the State Museum collections, it can be stated that Wynkoop's initials were also mounted on the scabbard in diamond chips. The latter sword was presented in the same year to George Campbell Wynkoop of the same regiment by the citizens of Pottsville. Blade 34"; sword 40"; overall 41"

Courtesy: Schuylkill County Historical Society

PART II

Sword Makers of the

Philadelphia Area

---

and others involved in the trade

Authors: Iris Wood
John Giblin

under the direction of

Bruce Bazelon

Pennsylvania Historical and Museum Commission

Preface to Part II

Over the past thirty years, or more, the Rose family of Blockley Township, as well as others concerned with the sword making trade, have presented an enigma to American sword collectors. While the importance, and some of the scale, of this sword-making activity is confirmed by recorded contracts of the early nineteenth century, as well as an appreciable number of surviving weapons, little has been known of details regarding the activities, or even the exact location, of the craftsmen involved. This lack of precise information was enhanced by the scanty nature, and sometimes absence, of listings regarding the firms within the Philadelphia directories of the period.

In the summer of 1985, the curtain of mystery enshrouding the Rose family, and others, began to be lifted. A research team, under the direction of Bruce Bazelon of the Pennsylvania Historical and Museum Commission, *undertook a search of primary records and documents. The diligence of team members Iris Wood and John Giblin was highly successful and, by summer's end, an incredible storehouse of details regarding the business of making swords in early 19th century Philadelphia had unfolded. The results follow.*

Andrew Mowbray —Publisher and Editor, *Man at Arms* magazine

HARVEY LEWIS

Although there were a number of swordsmiths that could make a sword from start to finish, many swordmakers either were not capable or didn't have the time to design their own patterns. This was especially true of the more complicated presentation swords. Occasionally, a contractor would hire an overall designer to coordinate the engraving or artwork with the actual forging of the pieces. This was Harvey Lewis's place in swordmaking.

Lewis was best known as a silversmith, first as a partner in the company of "Lewis and Smith" at 2 South Second Street until 1811 and then on his own at 143 Chestnut Street in 1824.[1] From the information we've now collected, we believe he was fairly well known at the time because of the number of swords he designed, including Winfield Scott's, Capt. Lewis Warrington's and the Watmough presentation sword.[2]*

While Lewis was the designer of the sword, he was not the organizer behind these contracts. They are all linked to General Thomas Cadwalader who directed the making of all three swords. He is also the one who picked Harvey Lewis for the contract.[3] He acted as a sort of middle-man between the Virginia Assembly and Harvey Lewis on the Scott sword and between Gaines and Lewis on the Watmough sword. On the Scott sword, he even turned down Gen. Scott's suggestion that the company of Fletcher and Gardiner be given the contract. Instead, Cadwalader gave the contract to his old friend, Harvey Lewis.[4] All these swords, according to Katharine McClinton, were finished around April 5, 1825. The Scott sword cost the Virginia Commonwealth $500.[5]

Very little is known about Lewis besides his link to the presentation swords. In the Pennsylvania Census of 1830, he is recorded as living in the High Street Ward of Philadelphia County and having 1 male 15-20 years of age, 3 males 40-50 years of age, 3 females under 5 years of age, 1 female 5-10 years of age, 1 female 15-20 years of age, 1 female 20-30 years of age, and 1 female 40-50 years of age living in his household.[6] He also had 1 freed colored female 10-24 years of age in the house. Total inhabitants were 12.[7]

In 1835, he recorded his will, leaving $700 to his niece Elizabeth Holtzbecker and $300 to her two brothers. He gave her another $300 for helping with his wife's illness.[8] From these amounts given, it can be assumed that he was financially secure, leaving no debts. His will even covered his burial. In the will he names his wife Elizabeth and three children; Rachel, Elizabeth and Mary.[9] At one point he

* See pages 20 and 21.

even loaned Lewis and George Holtzbecker $2,000 showing his apparent wealth.[10]

Our proof that Harvey Lewis is the maker of the Watmough sword comes from the Pennsylvania Inquirer article that appeared in Watmough's "... Statement of Sufferings and Services of Col. John G. Watmough ...", when he was running for Congress. In that article, Lewis is named as the artist.[11] By this term we assume they mean designer, knowing that Rose, Meer and Hub did the actual work. Lewis and his works began to fade out of the picture after 1835.

Notes

1 Stephen G.C. Ensko, *American Silversmiths and Their Marks*, N.Y.: Privately Printed, 1927, pg. 143.

2 Katharine M. McClinton, *Collecting American 19th Century Silver*, N.Y.: Bonanza Books, pg. 159.

3 McClinton; p. 159.

4 McClinton; p. 159.

5 McClinton; p. 159.

6 *Population Schedule of the Fifth Census of the U.S. — 1830.* Roll 159, Micro #m-19, pg. 49.

7 *Ibid;* pg. 49.

8 Harvey Lewis, *Will — 1835,* No. 150, Will No. 11, pg. 525.

9 Lewis; p. 525.

10 Lewis; p. 525.

11 *An Appeal to the People Being a Brief Statement of the Service and Sufferings of Col. John G. Watmough Now Before Them as a Candidate for the Twenty-Second Congress,* 1830, pg. 12.

WM. JOHN MEER, SR.
175?-1834

John Meer, born in the 1750's,[1] had a varied career as artist, engraver, and tavern owner.[2] The first public record of his activities was as an exhibitor at Charles Willson Peale's Columbianum in 1795.[3] He was listed in the exhibit catalog as a Japan painter. He was an exhibitor, but not a member of this new art organization. Tench Coxe was also listed as an exhibitor at the Columbianum.

John Meer became a naturalized citizen of the U.S. in February of 1798.[4] He was listed as a native of Birmingham, England. Initials on the exterior of the folded document appear to read "J. W. Meer".

The 1800 Census listed Meer as a painter in the North Ward of the city. The eleven members of his family were as follows: one male 27-45, one male 17-26, two males under 10, one female 27-45, one female 17-26, two females 11-16, and three females under 10.[5]

Meer bought his residence in 1805. The corner lot was situated on the west side of Delaware Seventh Street. The dwelling was described as a messuage.[6] On one line of the deed, the new owner is listed as "Wm. John Meer". The city directories of 1808, 1810, and 1820 list John Meer as an artist at this residence at 4 South Seventh Street.[7]

Meer became a Master Mason in Montgomery Lodge No. 19 of Philadelphia on April 18, 1807. As a Mason and artist, Meer decorated Masonic aprons. Some of these could have been done as early as 1800, but it is more likely that they were done after he became a Mason. One apron in particular definitely dates from 1820; it is signed "Meer / Philada / 1820". This apron and another decorated by Meer are currently in the collection of the Museum of Our National Heritage in Lexington, Massachusetts.[8]

In 1817-1818, Meer served as keeper of weights and measures for the city of Philadelphia.[9]

Meer was one of the earliest experimenters in engraving on stone. This he started in 1824.[10] He was listed in the city directory of 1825 as an "artist & inventor & manufacturer of Unique Razor Strops & Columbia Hones", again at 4 South Seventh Street.[11] These "Columbia Hones" may have been sharpening stones with patriotic designs engraved on them.

In 1830, Meer exhibited engravings for the last time at Peale's Pennsylvania Academy of the Fine Arts.[12]

Meer died in 1834 without a will. His widow Sarah administered his estate. An inventory was taken of his house.[13] The artist had an extensive library of over one thousand volumes and many paintings and engravings. In his library were found "tools, medalions, devices, and books of pattern buttons". Also there were found "razors, one box pattern razor strops, an instrument for striking ovals, and three silver medals". The enterprising artist operated a bar room, also. Some items which may have been work-in-progress included thirteen Masonic aprons, two Masonic apron cases, and two sword blades.

Meer's belongings were auctioned because expenses were listed for transporting "Goods to Auction Room" and "Postage of Books to Auction". This sale may not have resulted in much income because Mrs. Meer had debts that "are bad and cannot be realized".

Notes

1 *American Geneological Index.*

2 George C. Groce, David H. Wallace, *New York Historical Society Dictionary of Artists in America 1564-1860,* New Haven & London: Yale University Press, 1957, p. 437.

3 Charles Coleman Sellers, *Charles Willson Peale Later Life,* Vol. 23, Pt. II, Philadelphia: American Philosophic Society, 1947, p. 73.

4 Pennsylvania Archives Microfilm, Pa. Supreme Court Naturalization Papers, RG-33, Pos. Roll #2, 2/19/1798 - 5/8/1799.

5 U.S. Septennial Census, 1800, p. 79, reel 9, roll 43, vol. 9, #472.

6 Two deeds cover this transaction: Philadelphia Deed Book #EF 19, p. 537; and Bk. #EF 22, p. 241.

7 Philadelphia Pa. Directory, 1808, No. 1088:2, James Robinson, W. Woodhouse. Phila. Pa. Directory, 1810, No. 1090: 2, I -P, James Robinson. Phila. Directory & Register, 1820, No. 1102 -1, 3 -6, by Edward Whiteby, McCarty & Davis.

8 Barbara Franco, *Bespangled Painted & Embroidered,* Lexington, Mass.: Museum of Our National Heritage, 1980, p. 60.

9 Groce.

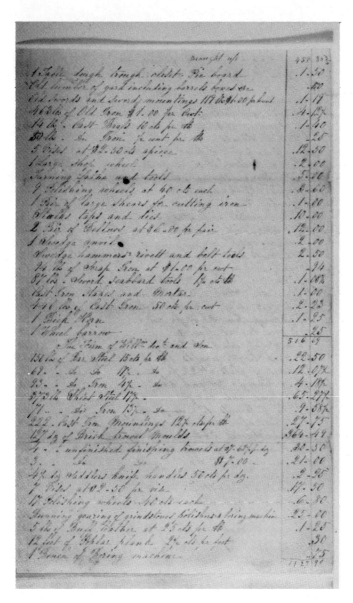

10 Groce.

11 Philadelphia Directory & Stranger's Guide, 1825, No. 1108 1-2, Thomas Wilson, John Bioren.

12 Groce.

13 Philadelphia City Hall, Administration #0, p. 139, #216.

LEWIS PRAHL
175?-1809

According to the *American Genealogical Index*, Lewis Prahl was born in the 1750's.[1]

In his book, *The American Sword,* Harold Peterson lists three United States contracts with Prahl.[2] A 1775 contract was for muskets and pikes. One of these pikes, which Prahl marked, is listed and illustrated in *Swords and Blades of the American Revolution.*[3] A 1776 contract was placed for 1,000 horsemen's sabers. And a 1781 contract was for 108 horsemen's swords costing 60 to 70 shillings each. That contract also included 23 bayonets.

These contracts apparently kept Prahl very busy because on March 13, 1777, he petitioned the Continental Congress for the release of 2 new recruits, Stephen Smith and John Bry. Both were skilled in the faro business and Prahl wished for them to work for him during the time they were supposed to be serving in the army. He stated in the letter that he had been and still was engaged by "the Council of Safety of the State of Pennsylvania in making Fire Arms for the use of the Continental Army."[4]

In 1782, Prahl resided in Blockley Twp. His occupation as a Smith was valued at 100 pounds in the Supply Tax of that year. His shop and tent were valued at 250 pounds; and his house and lot at 400 pounds. His total worth was 750 pounds.[5]

Listed as a blacksmith, Prahl bought a property in 1784 on W. Marlborough St. in Kensington in Northern Liberties Ward of Philadelphia County for 100 pounds.[6]

According to the 1790 census, Prahl was the only male over 16 in his family. Two males under 16 and three females were members of the households.[7]

For his work, Prahl ordered materials in 1790 from Tench Coxe who in turn placed the order with Johes and Lowers.

In the city directory, Prahl is listed as a blacksmith at 13 Wood St. in 1791,[9] and a whitesmith at 16 Knuckle St. in 1793.[10]

Prahl bought two other properties in the N. Liberties Ward in 1793: one on E. Delaware and 3rd St., the other at E. Delaware and 2nd St.[11] These two properties must have been between 461 and 467 N. 2nd St. because, according to Peterson, Prahl is listed as a gunsmith between those addresses in a 1795 directory."[12]

In 1800, Prahl bought yet another property from a goldsmith named John Brown. Prahl was listed as a blacksmith for the purchase of this E. Del. 2nd St. lot.[13] But in the 1800 List of Taxable Inhabitants, he is listed as a whitesmith in No. Liberties East Ward.[14]

Opposite: An all brass-hilted cavalry saber of a type frequently attributed to Prahl. The style of these weapons is considered uniquely that of the Philadelphia area.

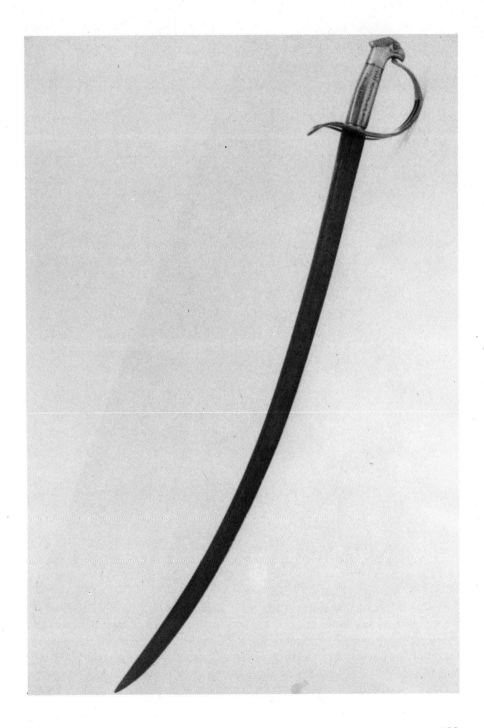

Lewis Prahl made his will in 1805. The whitesmith made a simple document. His wife Sophia was named as Executor and sole heir. In the event of her death, the estate would pass to their four children: Lewis, Sarah, Elizabeth and Samuel.[15] Prahl lived through 1809 when he was listed in the city directory as a cutler at 465 N. 2nd St.[16] By the following year, only his widow was listed at that address.[17]

Confusion exists in the 1814 administration of Prahl's will. Sophia Prahl,

104

"mother of the said Dec'd," " belives that Lewis Prahl, late Armourer at Fort Mifflin died without a will", and that the total value of his estate does "not in value exceed the sum of $108."[18] The illiterate Sophia then scribed her mark on the document.

A second document in the probate packet bears the same date and lists Sophia *widow*, blacksmith Samuel Prahl (son of the couple) and a third individual as owing the state $216 and an administration account that was to be reviewed by the Orphan's court. This obligation would be void if a will were found. The sole remaining items in the package are a detailed accounting of Prahl's funeral expenses.

No inventory was made and the will was never discovered because, in 1817, Orphan Court records list Samuel Prahl, Sarah Prahl and Elizabeth Wilson, all over 30 years of age, as "the only legitimate heirs at law of Lewis Prahl deceased late of the army of the United States."[19] Apparently, by this time, the widow Sophia and son Lewis had died.

Notes

1 *American Geneological Index.*
2 Harold L. Peterson, *The American Sword: 1775-1945.* Philadelphia: Ray Riling Arms Book Co., 1965, pg. X, 47.
3 George C. Neumann, *Swords and Blades of the American Revolution,* Harrisburg: Stackpole Books, 1973, pg. 212.
4 *National Archives Microfilm,* M247, r55, i42, v6, pg. 140.
5 *Supply Tax Summary,* Philadelphia Co., 1782.
6 *Philadelphia Deed Book,* No. D9, pg. 476.
7 *1st U.S. Census: Heads of Families — 1790, Pennsylvania,* pg. 202.
8 Historical Society of Pa., Manuscript file, *Tench Coxe Section — Coxe Papers,* Box 54 — Incoming Correspondence, Jan. 17, 1790, and Feb. 8, 1790.
9 *Philadelphia Pa. Directory,* 1791, No. 1069:1-2, Clement Biddle.
10 *Philadelphia Directory and Register,* 1793, No. 1070:1, James Hardie; 2, Dobson, p. 115.
11 *Philadelphia Deed Book,* No. D787, pg. 104; *Philadelphia Deed Book,* No. D69, pg. 239.
12 Peterson: p. 262.
13 *Philadelphia Deed Book,* IC16, pg. 128.
14 *List of Taxable Inhabitants — 1800,* Phil. 51-277, Roll 2937, No. 1101.
15 Philadelphia Will Book — No. 2, No. 44, p. 288.
16 *Philadelphia Directory — 1809,* No. 1089: 4, T-2 Appendix Pt. 1, James Robinson.
17 *Philadelphia Directory — 1810,* No. 1090:2, I-P, p. 225.

William Rose
1754-1810
(original)

The William Rose who founded the Rose family of swordmakers was born in 1754 in Philadelphia.[1] His wife, who was born in Wilmington, was Hannah Sellers.[2] The Roses had nine children between 1778 and 1800, six boys and three girls. One of the boys did not survive childhood. Three of the sons were to follow their father in his line of work: Joseph, William, and Benjamin F.

In the Supply Tax of 1782, Rose is listed as a smith in Blockley township. His occupation was valued at fifty pounds, his two houses at fourteen pounds, and his two cows at eight pounds for a total of seventy-two pounds.[3]

The 1790 Census of Blockley listed the members of the William Rose household as two males over sixteen, four males under sixteen, and three females.[4]

In the U.S. Direct Tax of 1798, William Rose was listed as owner and occupant of his property. The one acre lot with one dwelling house and two out houses was originally valued at six hundred dollars, but was later revised to six hundred and seventy-five dollars.[5]

The other buildings on his property were valued at twenty-eight hundred dollars and were described as: a 20 by 30 foot frame barn, a 12 by 41 foot old frame saw mill, a 20 by 15 foot log smith shop, a 23 by 30 foot stone blade mill, and a 41 by 23 stone tilt mill.[6]

According to the *Cyclopedia of Useful Arts,* in the tilt mill "a rude steel rod is stretched and fashioned into an even, smooth, and sharp-edged prism".[7] The tilt hammer falls with great force on the anvil at over one hundred strokes per minute. Because the anvil is level with the floor, the workman is seated in a pit; he is assisted by two boys who bring him the unfinished steel and remove the finished product. Rose's sons were undoubtedly his assistants and thus learned their father's skills.

The 1800 List of Taxable Inhabitants listed William Rose as a smith in Blockley.[8] The Census of that year enumerated the Rose household thus: one male 45 and up, five males 17-26, three males 11-16, one male under ten, two females 27-45, one female 17-26, one female 11-16, and one female under ten.[9]

In *The American Sword,* Harold Peterson reported a Rose federal contract. Dated December 9, 1807, and signed by Tench Coxe, Purveyor of Public Supplies, the contract was for 2,000 horsemen's sabers at $5.12½ each.[10]

Due to Rose's death on March 19, 1810, the 1810 Census lists the widow Hannah Rose as head of the surviving thirteen member family.[11]

Reminiscent of sword styles of the mid-18th century, this handsome and well made hanger would have been suitable for use by a non-commissioned officer of militia artillery. The urn-pommelled hilt is of brass; the grip of dark wood. The sword may date from the 1790's. (Mowbray collection)

William Rose's estate was inventoried following his death. Hannah Rose and her sons Joseph and William administered the proceedings. They were assisted by a William Warner, farmer, and John Frailey, wheelwright.[12] According to the Rose Bible records, Frailey was either the father-in-law or the brother-in-law of William Rose, the son.

In the administration papers, the deceased William Rose was described as a cutler as were his sons. The inventory gives a clear accounting of just how extensive their trade was. Among the tools in the listing were:

> 4 wrought iron tilt hammers — 15.00
> 4 tilt hammers — 8.00

These items would have been used in the previously-mentioned tilt mill. Also:

> bayonet swages — 4.00
> __iron & bayonet swage — 6.00
> 2 lots of smith tools — 3.25
> upright reamer — 1.00

There are also various listings of polishers, vices, anvils, hammers, tongs, bellows, and sheet iron stoves. Materials listed include:

> 16 lbs. drawed steel — 4.00
> lot of steel — 4.00
> 3 lots of old iron — 21.75
> 2 lumps of iron — 2.50
> lot of old brass — 1.00
> 332 lbs. of __wood — 16.60

Remaining products of his business included:

> lg. quant. horsemen's swords, unfinished — 250.00
> 225 sword blades — 81.00
> a lot of swords & sword blades — 18.00
> 1 horseman's sword — 2.50
> lot of bayonets — 6.00
> 18 gun barrels — 1.86
> 40 ramrods — 12.00
> lot of cutters — 10.00
> 2 pr. of small shears — 3.00
> lg. pr. of shears — 2.00

Notes

[1] Historical Society of Pennsylvania, third floor, Bible records — GSP Collection, Rose Bible Records 1754-1895 was the source of all birth and death dates.

[2] Christine Rose, Certified Genealogist, San Jose, California, provided Hannah Rose's maiden name.

[3] Supply Tax Summary, Philadelphia County, 1782, Microfilm at Pennsylvania Archives, Harrisburg.

[4] First U.S. Census, 1790, Heads of Families in Pennsylvania, p. 194

[5] U.S. Direct Tax of 1798: Tax List Pa., First Direct Tax Division, Third Assessment, Roll #3, Micro #372, D-102 (0051), Pa. Archives.

[6] _____, B-85 (0037).

[7] *Cyclopedia of Useful Arts* Vol. II, ed. Charles Tomlinson, New York: George Virtue & Co., p. 92.

[8] 1800 List of Taxable Inhabitants, original at H.S.P., LDS Microfilm, Phila 51-277, roll 2937, #168.

[9] Pennsylvania in 1800 Census, reel 8, p. 57, roll 42, vol. 8.

[10] Harold Peterson, *The American Sword,* Ray Riling Arms Book Co., 1965, p. 24.

[11] Pennsylvania in 1810 Census.

[12] Philadelphia City Hall, Administration #K, p. 379, #67.

JOSEPH ROSE
1778-1819

Joseph Rose, son of the original William Rose, sword-maker, was born on December 20, 1778.[1] He followed in his father's line of work. According to

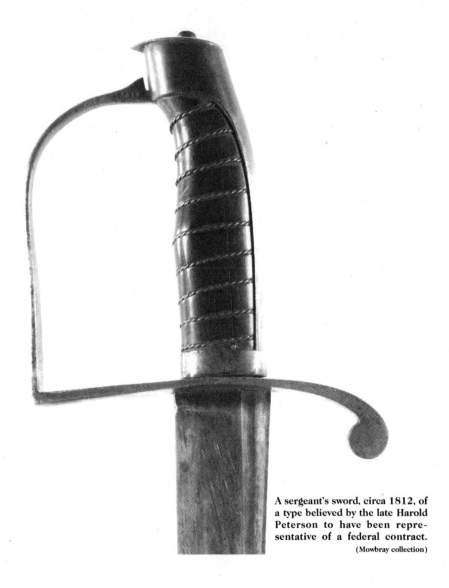

A sergeant's sword, circa 1812, of a type believed by the late Harold Peterson to have been representative of a federal contract.
(Mowbray collection)

Peterson, he had a federal contract for sergeant's swords in 1812.[2] He and his brothers William and Benjamin F. bought a property in 1815.[3] Although Joseph died on September 27, 1819, he was listed in the city directory of 1820 with his brother William as "Surgeon's Instrument Makers" in Hamilton Village.[4]

Notes

[1] Historical Society of Pennsylvania, third floor, Bible records — GSP Collection, Rose Bible Records 1754-1895.

[2] Harold Peterson, *The American Sword,* Ray Riling Arms Co., 1965, p. 105.

[3] Philadelphia Deed Book #MR22, p. 14.

[4] Philadelphia Directory & Register, 1820, No. 1102 — 1, 3-6, by Edward Whitely, McCarty & Davis.

WILLIAM ROSE SR.
1783-1854

William Rose Sr. was the son of the original swordmaker William Rose. He was born on February 23, 1783, in Blockley township. In 1807, he married

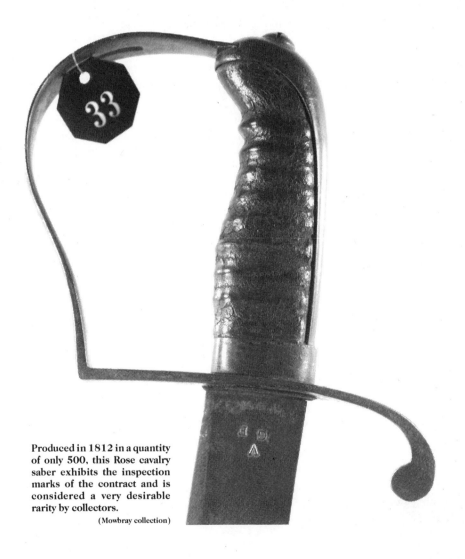

Produced in 1812 in a quantity of only 500, this Rose cavalry saber exhibits the inspection marks of the contract and is considered a very desirable rarity by collectors.

(Mowbray collection)

Susannah Frailey of Germantown. They had five children, three girls and two boys.[1] One of the sons, William, followed in his father's business.

In the 1810 Census of Blockley, Rose's household consisted of one male under 45, two males under 26, one male under 10, one female under 26, and one female under 10.[2]

Harold Peterson listed a federal contract with William Rose dated March 1812 for 500 horsemen's sabers with iron scabbards.[3]

In September of 1815, William and his brothers Joseph and Benjamin F. bought a property in Blockley. Listed as cutlers on the deed, they bought the northern moiety of a tract of ten acres including woodland and quarry ground.[4] This piece of ground is outlined and marked "W. Rose" on an old Philadelphia map.[5]

William Rose was listed with his brother Joseph in the city directory of 1820 as "Surgeon's Instrument Makers" in Hamilton Village.[6] Hamilton Village adjoins the lot of ground which the brothers had purchased.

Rose's wife and an infant son died in December of 1817. He remarried in 1820 to another Frailey from Germantown; her name was Catherine. According to the Bible records, she was not a sister to the first wife, but any other relationship is unknown at this point. This union resulted in ten children, only five of whom survived infancy. One of the boys that survived was named for his uncle Joseph the swordmaker.

The 1830 Blockley census listing has the members of the William Rose household as one male 40-50, two males 20-30, one male 15-20, three males 5-10, two males under 5, one female 30-40, two females 15-20, and one female under 5.[7]

Rose's second wife died in 1834. Sometime between then and 1836 he took another wife, Sophia Williamson. No date was listed for their marriage. They had four children: three girls and one boy; the boy did not survive infancy.

The city directories of 1839 and 1840 have William Rose listed as a cutler in Washington, West Philadelphia.[8] This indicates either a move or a change from Blockley's status as a township to that of being a part of the city.

The 1840 Census has the first listing of William Rose with a Senior attached to his name. The Rose Senior household in West Philadelphia included one male 50-60, one male 30-40, one male 20-30, two males 15-20, one male 10-15, one female 40-50, one female 10-15, one female 5-10, and two females under 5.[9]

The 1850 Census lists more detailed information than those done previously. The William Rose household consisted of the sixty-seven year old cutler; Sophia, age 54; Joseph, age 26, cutler; twenty-four year old Rudolph F.; twenty-two year old John W.; eighteen year old Suzanna F.; fourteen year old Anna S.; twelve year old Mary; and seven year old Elvira H.[10]

One of a number of blade marks (on the spine near the grip) to be found on swords made by the family of Rose.

William Rose Senior died on January 29, 1854, at the age of seventy. Leonard Frailey, Rose's brother-in-law by his first marriage, acted as administrator of the estate at the request of Rose's widow.[11] Rudolph F. Rose, son by Rose's second wife, assisted in the administration. Inventories were taken of both William Rose Sr.'s estate and the Firm of William Rose & Son. The listing of Rose's personal property included:

> Old swords & Sword mountings 119 lbs. @ $1.00 per hund. — 1.19
> 463 lbs. of Old Iron $1.00 per cwt. — 4.12½
> 14 lbs. of Cast Brass 10 cts per lb. — 1.40
> 50 lbs. of Cast Iron ½ cent per lb. — .25
> 94 lbs. of Scrap Iron at $1.00 per cwt. — .94
> 87 lbs. of Sword Scabbard tools 1¼ cts lb. — 1.08¼
> 446 lbs. of Cast Iron 50 cts per cwt. — 2.23
> 5 Vises at $2.50 cts a piece — 12.50
> 1 lg. shop wheel — 2.00
> 9 polishing wheels at 40 cts each — 3.60
> 1 pr lg shears for cutting iron — 1.00
> Stalks taps & dies — 10.00
> 2 pr of Bellows at $6 per pair — 12.00
> 1 Swedge anvil — 2.00
> Swedge hammers rivett & bolt tools — 2.50

The accounting of the firm of William Rose & Son listed:

> 150 lbs. Bar Steel — 22.50
> 69 lbs. Bar Steel — 12.07½
> 93 lbs. Iron — 4.18½
> 373 lbs. Sheet Steel — 65.27½
> 71 lbs. Iron — 9.58½
> 222 Cast Iron Mountings — 27.75
> 5 lbs. Buff leather — 1.25
> 107 Ferrules — 1.33¼
> 470 lbs. scrap sheet steel — 4.18
> 183 lbs. scrap steel — 1.22
> 167 lbs. scrap iron — 1.25

484 lbs. scrap iron — 4.84
987½ lbs. cast iron — 4.93¼
261 lbs. wrought scrap — 6.52
29 lbs. old scrap iron — .29
68 lbs. old scrap iron — .68
Old scrap steel chunks — 2.00

In addition, many tools were listed. Listings of many trowels and trowel molds indicate the diversity of the firm's work. Finally, the Rose's "old work shop" was valued at $125.00.

William Rose Sr.'s widow Sophia died in 1858.

Notes

1 Historical Society of Pennsylvania, third floor, Bible records — GSP Collection, Rose Bible Records 1754-1895 was the source for all birth and death dates.

2 Population Schedule of the Third Census of the U.S., 1810, Microcopy 252, Roll 56, p. 74.

3 Harold Peterson, *The American Sword,* Ray Riling Arms Co., 1965, p. 28.

4 Philadelphia Deed Book #MR22, p. 14.

5 Philadelphia City Map, Pennsylvania Archives, Harrisburg.

6 Philadelphia Directory & Register, 1820, No. 1102 -1, 3 -6, by Edward Whitely, McCarty & Davis.

7 Fifth Census of the U.S., 1830, Pa. Vol. 16, Microcopy #19, Roll 158, p. 20.

8 M'Elroy's Philadelphia, Pa. Directory, A. M'Elroy, Issac Ashmead & Co., 1839, No. 1124:3, and 1840, No. 1125:3.

9 Sixth Census of the U.S., 1840, Microcopy No. 704, Roll 489, Philadelphia County, p. 180, Pa. Vol. 25.

10 Seventh Census of the U.S., 1850, Microcopy No. 432, Roll 823, Philadelphia County, p. 501.

11 Philadelphia City Hall, Administration #Q, p. 243, #49.

BENJAMIN F. ROSE
178?-18??

Benjamin F. Rose, son of the original William Rose swordmaker, was born in the month of October. His Bible record is incomplete but it does indicate that his year of birth was sometime between 1783 and 1788.[1] In 1815, he bought a property with his brothers Joseph and William.[2] In 1825, Benjamin F. was listed in the city directory as a cutler at 33 North Tenth Street.[3] No date of death has been found for Benjamin F. Rose.

One of a number of highly ornate swords made by the Rose firm for Congressional presentation to heroes of the War of 1812; possibly by Joseph, Benjamin and William Rose, Sr., working in collaboration.

Notes
[1] Historical Society of Pennsylvania, third floor, Bible records — GSP Collection, Rose Bible Records 1754-1895.
[2] Philadelphia Deed Book #MR 22, p. 14.
[3] Philadelphia Directory & Stranger's Guide, 1825, No. 1108 1-2, Thomas Wilson, John Bioren.

WILLIAM ROSE JR.
1810-1883

William Rose Jr., son of William Sr., was born March 24, 1810.[1] He must have been named after his grandfather who died five days earlier. He followed the family tradition of the cutler's trade.

In the 1840 city directory, he is listed as a cutler in Washington, West Philadelphia.[2] The census that year listed his household members: one male 30-40, one female 30-40, one female 20-30, and one female under 5.[3]

The 1850 Census listed the household members by name: William Jr., 40, cutler; Jane F., 39; Margueretta, 12; John F., 10; Isabel Shule, 85, from Delaware; John Coxey, 22, cutler; and George Ezxey, 18, cutler.[4] The last two were undoubtedly workers for him.

Although the firm of William Rose and Son had been inventoried at the death of Rose Sr., the firm may not have gone out of business. William Jr. may have carried on the firm's name. One indication of this possibility can be found in Katherine Morrison McClinton's *Collecting American Nineteenth Century Silver*. In the chapter on presentation swords, she states that "at the exhibit of the Metropolitan Fair in New York City in April, 1864, presentation swords were displayed by the following companies: . . . William Rose & Sons."[5]

William Rose Jr. died on September 28, 1883.

Notes

[1] Historical Society of Pennsylvania, third floor, Bible records — GSP Collection, Rose Bible Records 1754-1895.

[2] M'Elroy's Philadelphia, Pennsylvania Directory, 1840, No. 1125: 3, A. M'Elroy, Issac Ashmead & Co.

[3] Sixth Census of the U.S., 1840, Microcopy 704, Roll 489, Pa. Vol. 25, p. 180.

[4] Seventh Census of the U.S., 1850, Microcopy #432, Roll 823, Philadelphia Co., p. 502.

[5] Katherine Morrison McClinton, *Collecting American Nineteenth Century Silver*, New York: Bonanza Books, p. 169-170.

JOSEPH ROSE
1823-1881

Joseph Rose, son of William Rose Sr., was born September 29, 1823. He lived until June 5, 1881.[1] No records have been found to indicate that he was a cutler or swordmaker by trade. His dates are mentioned because of Peterson's book. Peterson said that a Joseph Rose made naval presentation swords in the 1830 to 1840 period.[2] This swordmaker could not have been the Joseph who was the son of the original William because he had died in 1819; nor is it likely that he was this Joseph, son of William Sr. This Joseph would have been too young to be working in the 1830's. This indicates that Peterson must have been wrong in assigning his dates.

Notes

[1] Historical Society of Pennsylvania, third floor, Bible records — GSP Collection, Rose Bible Records 1754-1895.
[2] Harold Peterson, *The American Sword*, Ray Riling Arms Co., 1965, p. 196.

EMMOR TREGO WEAVER

Emmor Trego Weaver was a silversmith, watchcase maker, gilder, jeweler and swordsmith from 1808-1820 in the Philadelphia area. Originally from the Chester Co. area, he was the son of Joshua and Mary (Trego) Weaver and was born July 6, 1786, in Philadelphia.[1]

While it is Weaver's swords that are of importance to this article (despite their poor quality), he was most noted as a jeweler and his specialty was Masonic Lodge pins and other emblems. He is listed in the Philadelphia city Directories from 1809-1830. In 1809, he is listed as a gold and silver watchcase maker at 17 Elfreth Alley.[2] By 1810, he has moved his business to the Lower Delaware Ward of Philadelphia as a silversmith and jeweler with a small family to support: 1 male under 26 years of age, (probably Weaver), 1 female under 26 years of age (his wife, Mary Boswell Weaver), and 1 female under 10 years of age.[3] His wife, Mary Weaver, was the daughter of William and Elizabeth Boswell. She was born April 17, 1786, in Salem, Ohio. They were married January 29, 1807.[4]

By 1820, Weaver's family had grown and changed, and so had his business. In the 1820 Census, he was listed as having living in his household, 4 males under 10 years of age, 1 female 11-16 years of age, 1 male 27-45 years of age and 2 females 27-45 years of age.[5] In the Philadelphia City Directory for that year, Weaver is listed as a silversmith at 20 N. 4th and 1 Loxely Ct.[6] Apparently, he was either operating two separate businesses at this time or his business had grown so large that he needed another workshop.

In 1815, Weaver established Lodge #50 of the Free Masons at East Whitehead, Chester County, Pa., in February. By 1820-21, Weaver had established himself in some prominent social circles. After having joined the Masons and become very well known, he achieved the office of senior warden and master of Philadelphia Lodge #2. In 1826, he was elected the Lodge secretary.[7] It was also believed that he had helped to establish Lodge #1 of the Independent Order of Odd Fellows in conjunction with Thomas Wildley of Baltimore.[8]

In 1825, Weaver moved his business again to 73 North 3rd Street, and is listed in the Philadelphia City Directories as a Silversmith and Jeweler.[9] In 1829, he is listed in the directories as having moved to his permanent address of 11 North 4th Street in the High Street Ward of Philadelphia where he opened a large shop and factory.[10] It was through this shop that he, according to John Jodren's

Opposite: A silver-hilted ornamental infantry officers' sword of a type associated — many are so marked — to Emmor Trego Weaver. Being hilted in silver, the smith/cutler featured a light, and sometimes fragile, construction. The spoon-like development of the upper knuckleguard is uniquely attributed to Weaver. (Mowbray collection)

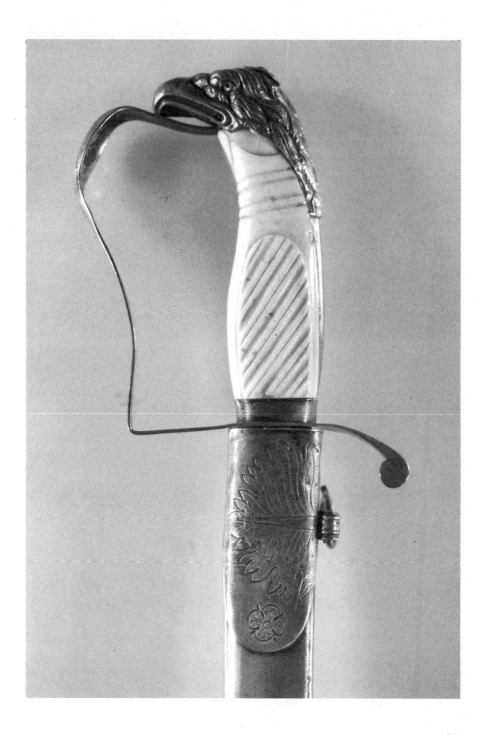

Encyclopedia of Pennsylvania Biographies, "advised and consulted with Benjamin Franklin, making the first lightening rod points in use."[11] It was also through this shop that Weaver took on the title of "Silversmith and Swordmaker".[12]

By 1830, Weaver's family had also grown again. According to the 1830 census from the High Street Ward, he had 1 male 5-10 yers of age, 2 males 10-15 years of age, 2 males 15-20 years of age, 1 male 20-30 years of age and 1 male 40-50 years of age. On the female side, 3 females under 5 years of age, 1 female 15-20 years of age and 1 female 40-50 years of age.[13] Of the children, only one ever rose to a personality of note. Emmor White Weaver, Emmor Trego's oldest son, was well educated in public and private school and became a well known Philadelphia businessman, being part-owner in the firm of Weaver and Sprankle.[14]

Weaver's swordmaking abilities were not very impressive. He used second rate imported German blades, poorly cast figureheads on the pommel, plain grips, and was even known to have used an old spoon cast to form his shell guards.

Notes

1 John W. Jordan, *Encyclopedia of Pennsylvania Biographies,* New York: Lewis Historical Publishing Co., 1921, Vol. 13, p. 220.

2 James Robinson, *Philadelphia Pa. Directory — 1809,* No. 1089:4, T-Z and Appendix pt. 1.

3 *Population Schedule of the Third Census of the U.S. — 1810,* Roll 55-Pennsylvania, Vol. 12- Philadelphia City, No. 17.

4 Jordan: pg. 220.

5 *Population Schedule of the Fourth Census of the U.S. — 1820,* Roll 108-Pennsylvania, Vol. 13, p. 253.

6 Edward Whitely, *Philadelphia Directory and Register — 1820,* No. 1102:1, 3-6, McCarty and Davis.

7 Jordan: pg. 220.

8 Jordan: pg. 220.

9 Thomas Wilson, *Philadelphia Directory and Stranger's Guide,* No. 1108:1-2, John Bioren.

10 Robert DeSilver, *DeSilver's Philadelphia Directory and Stranger's Guide,* No. 1111:1-3, James Maxwell.

11 Jordan: pg. 220.

12 Robert DeSilver, *DeSilver's Philadelphia Directory and Stranger's Guide,* No. 1111:1-3, James Maxwell.

13 *Population Schedule of the Fifth Census of the U.S. — 1830,* Roll 159, Vol. 17, No. 19, p. 47.

14 Jordan: pg. 220.

FREDERICK WILLIAM WIDMANN
178?-1848

Frederick William Widmann emigrated from Bremen in Germany to America in 1816. He was in his late twenties or early thirties. Arriving at the port of

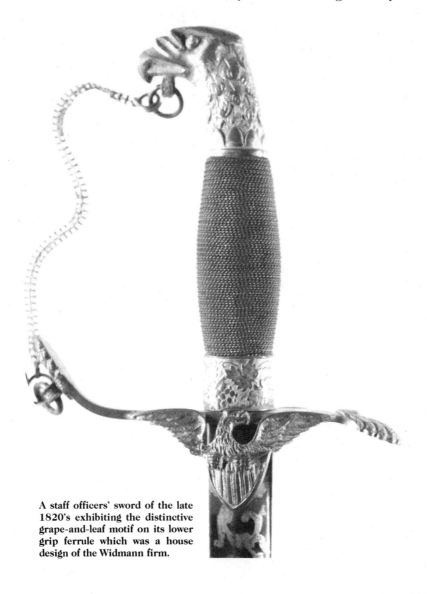

A staff officers' sword of the late 1820's exhibiting the distinctive grape-and-leaf motif on its lower grip ferrule which was a house design of the Widmann firm.

Philadelphia on October 23 aboard the Brig Hannah, his worldly possessions included a trunk, a knapsack, and four boxes of tools.[1]

Although he lived in the U.S. for over thirty years, Widmann never became fluent in speaking English. His 1846 will, written in German, had to be translated and certified by the Interpreter for the Commonwealth of Pennsylvania.[2]

No records of Widmann's whereabouts or activities are known from after his arrival here until 1828. In that year and in the following two years, he is listed in the city directories as an "ornamental sword mounter and die sinker" at 98 North Third Street.[3] Widmann remained there as a swordmaker through 1840 as the city directories attest.[4]

Although Widmann lived at this address for twenty years, he never owned the property. It was rented from a Henry Geisse. Widmann originally willed money to Geisse's children on the condition that his rent not be raised. But in a codicil to his will added in 1848, Widmann rescinded this bequest due to an increase in his rent.

Widman eluded being counted in the 1820 and 1840 Censuses, but he was counted in the 1830 Census of the Lower Delaware Ward. At that time he was in his forties. His household included another man in his forties, a young man between 15 and 20 years of age, and three women: one in her forties and two in their sixties.[5] None of these people, however, seem to be related to Widmann. The swordmaker had never married. His relatives lived in Germany and included his sister Eleanor Widmann of Breslau, his nephew Doctor Julius Widmann of Bremen, and several other children of his deceased brother.

According to his will, Widmann had a Mrs. Huntz and a Julius Knecke living in his house. Knecke was a workman for Widmann as was a Lewis Loemmel who was bequeathed design books, armorial designs, and a book on electro-galvanic gilding. Loemmel was eliminated from the will in the codicil. Because he is referred to as "having left me and my workshop," the man may have resided in Widmann's home. The intended inheritance for Loemmel was willed to a Jacob Weisser "who has been my apprentice."

A person named Brown was also mentioned in the will. But, "if Brown remains with me," fails to identify the man as either a workman or a member of the household or both. In the codicil, Widmann mentions another worker, John Hoffman, "who did not work with me when I wrote my last Will, but who is now again with me."

Widmann wished that his employees would continue his business without interruption after his death. If that was not possible, he preferred that his possessions be sold gradually rather than at auction, "else such articles as sword blades worth many dollars would have to be sacrificed for a mere trifle."

Opposite: A militia cavalry officers' saber by Widmann. The handsome stylized design of the eagle pommel was continued after Widmann's death by the firm of Horstmann who bought many of the cutler's fixtures.

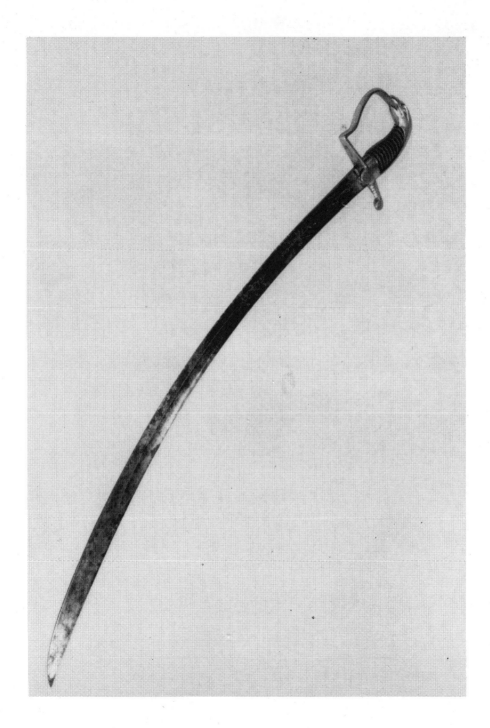

Detail of upper scabbard mounting showing the Widmann house mark as well as the distinctive grape-and-leaf motif unique to the firm.

Widmann also stipulated that, "Those two splendid swords, put in a case lined with velvet, are worth at least, the one $ 200 and the other $ 100," could be sold at half price if someone were interested in them.

Of his work materials, Widmann stipulated that the silver which he had bought from Mr. Horstmann could be sold back to him at the same price he had paid for it. The Horstmann firm is known to have bought the bulk of Widmann's business.[6]

Notes

1 National Archives Microfilm Publication, Micro No. 425, Passenger Lists of Vessels Arriving at Philadelphia 1800-1882, Roll 23, List 262.

2 Philadelphia Will Book #20, p. 203, no. 97.

3 DeSilver's Philadelphia Directory & Stranger's Guide, Robert DeSilver, James Maxwell, 1828, No. 1109: 1; 1829, No. 1110; and 1830, No. 1111, 1-3.

4 ____, 1836, and M'Elroy's Philadelphia Pa. Directory — 1840, no. 1125: 3, A. M'Elroy, Issac Ashmead & Co.

5 Fifth Census of the U.S., 1830, Penn. Vol. 17, Phil. City, Micro No. 19, Roll 159, p. 171.

6 Machine Book, Wm. H. Horstmann Co., 1842-1872, Entries 1848 shows the purchase of Widmann's sword business.

SOURCES

Published

John Brewer Brown: *Sword and Firearm Collection of the Society of the Cincinnati in the Anderson House Museum Washington D.C.* (Washington: Society of the Cincinnati, 1965)

Edwin A. Glover: *Bucktailed Wildcats* (New York: Thomas Yoseloff, 1960) 328 Pp.

Francis T. Miller: *The Photographic History of the Civil War* (New York: Review of Reviews, 1912) 10 volumes.

Francis B. Heitman: *Historical Register and Dictionary of the United States Army* (Washington: Government Printing Office, 1903) 2 volumes.

Francis B. Heitman: *Historical Register of Officers of the Continental Army* (Washington: The Rare Book Shop, 1914)

T. Thomas Scharf and Thompson Westcott: *History of Philadelphia 1609-1884* (Philadelphia: L.H. Everts, 1884) 3 volumes.

Frank H. Taylor: *Philadelphia in the Civil War 1861 1865* (Philadelphia: Published by the City, 1913) 360 Pp.

Ezra T. Warner: *Generals in Blue* (Louisiana State University, 1964) 680 Pp.

Samuel T. Wiley: *Biographical and Portrait Cyclopedia of Schuylkill County Pennsylvania* (Philadelphia: Rush, West and Company, 1893) 752 Pp.

Edwin Wolf 2nd: *Philadelphia Portrait of an American City* (Harrisburg: Stackpole Books, 1975) 351 Pp.

Manuscript

Pennsylvania State Archives. Record Group 26. Department of State, Secretary of the Commonwealth. "Commission Records for Officers of the Pennsylvania Militia and National Guard 1800-1940."

Pennsylvania State Archives. Record Group 19. Dept. of Military Affairs "Abstract Cards for Individual Records of the Civil War." "Abstract Cards for Individual Records of the National Guard of Pennsylvania 1865-1916."

Original correspondence and documents contained in the accession files of the various lending institutions.